Criminal Psychology

Criminal Psychology

Francis Pakes
and
Suzanne Pakes

WILLAN
PUBLISHING

Published by

Willan Publishing
Culmcott House
Mill Street, Uffculme
Cullompton, Devon
EX15 3AT, UK
Tel: +44(0)1884 840337
Fax: +44(0)1884 840251
e-mail: info@willanpublishing.co.uk
website: www.willanpublishing.co.uk

Published simultaneously in the USA and Canada by

Willan Publishing
c/o ISBS, 920 NE 58th Ave, Suite 300
Portland, Oregon 97213-3786, USA
Tel: +001(0)503 287 3093
Fax: +001(0)503 280 8832
e-mail: info@isbs.com
website: www.isbs.com

First published 2009

ISBN   978-1-84392-364-0 paperback
       978-1-84392-328-2 hardback

British Library Cataloguing-in-Publication Data

A catalogue record for this book is available from the British Library.

FSC
Mixed Sources
Product group from well-managed
forests and other controlled sources
Cert no. SGS-COC-2482
www.fsc.org
© 1996 Forest Stewardship Council

Project managed by Deer Park Productions, Tavistock, Devon
Typeset by GCS, Leighton Buzzard, Bedfordshire
Printed and bound by T.J. International Ltd, Padstow, Cornwall

Contents

List of illustrations and tables

Illustrations

Tables

Acknowledgements

The teaching of psychology is never dull. Criminal psychology is doubly interesting; the study of human behaviour at its most intriguing. Criminal psychology is an expanding area which involves contributions from psychology's greats, such as Freud, Bandura and Zimbardo. At the same time, it has currency and an applied cutting edge. Many findings influence criminal justice in practice, such as police interviewing or sentencing. It is theoretically vibrant and pragmatically successful. It is also fast moving, as criminal psychology develops alongside developments in criminal justice, mainstream psychology also is affected by advances in criminology, law and forensic science.

We have aimed to do justice to the unique position of criminal psychology: firmly footed in psychology, but placed in an exciting real life context. Apart from the key psychological approaches, studies and theories, this book also discusses key stages and issues in criminal justice. After all, only with a thorough knowledge of the setting to which criminal psychology is applied, can a rich and meaningful understanding of the area be gained.

We hope that that orientation will encourage students to develop career-oriented thinking. That is why the book contains eight interviews with criminal psychologists who work in various settings in criminal justice. Two of these combine research, teaching and consultancy as university lecturers. Another works in a mental hospital whereas yet another conducts research for the National Policing Improvement Agency. One psychologist interviewed is employed in a women's prison, whereas a colleague works with male offenders on long-term prison sentences. A psychologist working in probation explains the complexities of working with offenders whereas an area psychologist explains his role whenever there is a prison riot in one of the prisons on his watch. The contributions of these psychologists in profile emphasise that criminal psychology offers a rich variety of careers that can be both exciting and rewarding.

We thank Mick Lydon, media officer at HMP Wandsworth for his hospitality and the opportunity to take photographs at that establishment. These photos were taken by the first author. We thank Jacqui Lindsey at Medium Secure Unit Ravenswood House in Fareham for her contribution to 'Tom's story' in Chapter 5. Finally, we express our gratitude to Penny Crooks (Havant College, Hampshire), Becky Milne (University of Portsmouth), and Amanda Wood (The Portsmouth Grammar School) for their extensive and insightful comments on various parts of this book and to Evie Bentley and Jennifer Toal for comprehensively scrutinising an early draft.

This book is dedicated to our daughters Katie and Anna. Here's to curiosity.

Chapter 1

Crime: the phenomenon

Applying psychology to crime

Criminal psychology mainly seeks to answer two questions. The first is how can psychology further our understanding of crime, its causes, consequences and prevention? The second is how can psychology help the criminal justice system and other agencies in dealing with crime? Criminal psychology is an applied branch of psychology. That means that we seek to apply general psychology to issues of crime and justice.

There are three components to that. The first is that we apply the same research methods in order to understand offending behaviour and the behaviour of criminal justice officials. Secondly, many key studies in psychology have direct relevance to criminal psychology. That includes the Stanford Prison Experiment (Haney *et al.* 1973). That study in a simulated prison setting showed the importance of roles and expectations on how people in that setting behaved. It has direct relevance to understanding imprisonment. Another is Loftus and Palmer's eyewitness study that highlights how easily witnesses' memories are distorted due to information provided after the fact (1974). Finally, the approaches that characterise general psychology apply to criminal psychology as well.

The first section of this chapter will discuss these approaches and their relevance to criminal psychology. After that we turn to crime. We first discuss how the true rate of crime can be established. Then we look at what crime actually is and why certain behaviours are labelled crimes. The chapter ends by discussing fear of crime.

Drunk and disorderly. One in three arrested in England and Wales are under the influence of alcohol; two out of three have recently taken drugs.

Photo courtesy of Jan Brayley (Hampshire Constabulary).

Approaches in criminal psychology

Understanding criminal psychology involves assessing how the main psychological approaches apply to the applied field of criminal psychology. That should help you identify links to key issues in psychology and to position criminal psychology as a specialist area of psychology. In this section we will look at learning theory, psychodynamic theory, cognitive approaches, biological theory, and the social approach.

Learning theory

One way of explaining behaviour is to regard it as the product of learning. Criminal behaviour is no exception. There are several principles that underlie learning theory, such as operant and classical conditioning, imitation and modelling. Pavlov's salivating dog is the best example of *classical conditioning*, or learning by association (Pavlov 1927). It is not thought that classical conditioning has much to do with understanding how criminal behaviour is acquired. *Operant conditioning* on the other hand has more relevance. Operant conditioning is learning via trial and error (Skinner 1938). It occurs when behaviour is displayed and rewarded. That reinforcement increases the likelihood of such behaviour occurring again in the future.

Operant conditioning can play a role in the early learning processes involving antisocial behaviour: a person engages in some kind of behaviour, and finds that it is intrinsically rewarding. Or a youngster might discover that random acts of vandalism attract approval from peers.

Criminal behaviour is more susceptible to influences from social or observational learning. Witnessing violence can be a strong precursor to acquiring that behaviour. Bandura, Ross and Ross's (1961) famous Bobo-doll study is a classic involving the transmission of aggression from an adult model to young children. We discuss it fully as a key study in Chapter 2. But we will also look at how violent movies affect juveniles and adults and whether violent video games increase aggression as well. Such influences are often explained in terms of observational learning, or imitation.

Psychodynamic theory

Sigmund Freud pioneered the idea that behaviour is shaped by tension between innate drives and internalised social constraints. This was a key theme running through his psychodynamic approach. In the psychodynamic approach, our mental life is characterised by conflict between desire and restraint. Desires may well propel us towards crime. Stealing can be a way of obtaining nice things, whereas sexual crimes can help us satisfy deep seated and innate urges. But we do not always take what we want, or act on our hormones. Instead, we continually face an internal and largely subconscious struggle between our 'id', out to satisfy our every desire immediately, and our 'superego', our conscience which motivates us to obey the rules of society. The 'ego', our conscious mind, is in essence the battlefield between the 'id' and the 'superego' (Gross 2005).

In order to not be overwhelmed by that continuous state of conflict, the mind utilises so-called defence mechanisms. Defence mechanisms reduce stress and anxiety and are therefore said to be adaptive responses. A key one is *repression*, which means keeping unwanted thoughts out of consciousness to the point of completely forgetting them. Repression is a phenomenon we shall revisit when we discuss witness memory, in particularly when dealing with child sexual abuse that occurred a long time ago.

Aggression features heavily in Freud's work. Psychodynamic theory emphasises the role of dark forces when explaining aggression. Men are not gentle creatures, Freud warns us in *Civilization and its Discontents* from 1930. According to Freud, aggression is not exceptional human behaviour: if we were to let loose our 'id', aggression would be most commonplace:

Men are not gentle creatures, who want to be loved, who at the most can defend themselves if they are attacked; they are, on the contrary, creatures among whose instinctual endowments is to be reckoned a powerful share of aggressiveness. As a result, their neighbor is for them not only a potential helper or sexual object, but also someone who tempts them to satisfy their aggressiveness on him, to exploit his capacity for work without compensation, to use him sexually without his consent, to seize his possessions, to humiliate him, to cause him pain, to torture and to kill him. Homo hominy lupus [man is wolf to man]. (Freud 1930: 111)

Freud's perspective on aggression represents a rather pessimistic view on humanity. But do remember that Freud published this book in 1930. As a Jewish physician in Vienna in the 1930s he soon witnessed the rise of anti-Semitism and fascism. Freud and his family fled Austria to come to the UK to escape persecution. He died in London in 1939 and with hindsight, his work on human aggression was painfully predictive of the horrors of World War II.

Finally, Freud advanced the concept of *catharsis*, i.e. letting off steam. When frustration and tension are pent up in an individual, certain activities can serve to reduce that stress. It includes sports, laughter, but certain criminal offences can also be cathartic, and that might explain certain types of offences that might give the offender a cathartic adrenaline rush. Such offences can include vandalism and violence.

Psychodynamic theories are well suited to explain crime and antisocial behaviour. They look at the human soul as a place in which sinister forces are at work below a thin veneer of civilisation. Because of that, it is tempting to apply Freudian explanations to criminal behaviour. However, we must remember the criticisms levelled against Freud's school of thought. Freud did not experiment, but rather based his theories on subjective interpretations of case studies. In addition, Freud was a child of his time. He probably overemphasised the role of repressed sexuality because he lived in a time and place characterised by sexual inhibition. Thirdly, you might wonder whether Freud himself in his writing displayed one of his very own defence mechanisms, that of *projection*. Projection means that you attribute your own negative personality traits unto others, so that if you are mistrustful, you assume that everybody else is as well (Freud 1923). It is conceivable that Freud's bleak perspective on humanity has rather been informed by how he viewed himself.

Sweatbox. Offenders call it a sweatbox: the vehicle used for transporting prisoners.
Photo courtesy of Francis Pakes.

Cognitive approaches

Cognitive theory is concerned with how people interpret and organise information. It looks at how individuals use information and prior knowledge to make sense of the world around them. In the area of crime, cognitive theory is of relevance in a number of areas. Firstly, there is a link to aggression. It is well-known that aggressive scripts are acquired via witnessing aggressive behaviour. A script is a packet of knowledge that helps us organise the world and derive expectations and plans for action (Schank and Abelson 1977). Aggressive scripts are scripts that suggest that use of violence is the appropriate action in certain situations. It is also established that aggressive children tend to have weaknesses in how they read and respond to ambiguous social situations. That is an area where thinking patterns are of relevance as we shall see in Chapter 2.

The reliability of eyewitness testimony has been researched intensively from the cognitive perspective. It is well known that human memory does not act as if it is a DVD recorder that passively and accurately records all information. In fact, memory is an active, constructive process that is subject to distortion (Bartlett 1932). Furthermore, the way in which a witness is interviewed by the police can substantially facilitate or hamper effective and accurate recall. For that reason, the so-called cognitive interview has been developed in order to maximise the information that is obtained from witnesses via interviews (Milne and Bull 1999). Such research is vital for the administration of justice. This is an area that we will consider in detail in Chapter 3, Solving crime.

The cognitions of jurors are assessed in the area of courtroom psychology (see Chapter 4). Juror assumptions about human behaviour and their stereotypes as to which individuals might be criminal are an important area of study. Thus, cognitive theory informs criminal psychology in a variety of settings, varying from understanding the thinking patterns of the offender and the training of police officers about the intricacies of memory, to the decision making of jurors.

Biological theory

The extent to which our behaviour is determined by our biological make up is a controversial issue in criminal psychology. It is also difficult to assess. Crime is not a natural category but a diverse set of behaviours that for various reasons have been prohibited, as we shall see later. If crimes are a social category you would not assume that a biological theory would be able to further our understanding of crime very much. But that does not mean that there is no place for biological theories in criminal psychology. It has been established via brain scans that certain violent criminals show patterns of brain activity that are different from other people (Raine *et al*. 1997, see Chapter 2). In addition, a link has been established between Attention Deficit Hyperactivity Disorder (ADHD) in children, and later offending. ADHD is in part hereditary (Pratt *et al*. 2002). We will later discover via twin studies that a modest influence of genes on crime is not unlikely. Thus, to a limited degree, we can use biology and genetics to further our understanding of criminal behaviour.

It is, however, important to be aware of the caveats. Biology or genes by themselves do not explain human behaviour sufficiently. There is no such thing as a 'crime gene', nor is there an aggression gene, nor is there one particular genetic set of characteristics that make a life of crime inevitable. Such a view would be unjustifiably *reductionist*. Genes interact with each other and with the person's environment in complex ways, so that prediction becomes very difficult indeed: human behaviour is shaped by many factors. That said there are some areas where the exclusion of any influence of biological or genetic variables would be unduly restrictive.

Reductionism

Reductionism refers to the tendency to oversimplify the causes of human behaviour. If we ascribe the causes of behaviour to our biological or genetic make-up, we ignore many other factors. It is unlikely that criminal behaviour is always explained by the same one or two factors. It is likely to be much more complex than that so that an overly reductionist view on crime is likely to be inaccurate.

The social approach

We are social animals. Our behaviour is profoundly influenced by the behaviour of the people that surround us. The social approach has relevance for criminal psychology too. Much criminal behaviour is group behaviour and being part of a group affects the way we behave. Nowhere is this clearer as in the area of *deinviduation* (see Chapter 2). The jury is another closed group. There is no doubt that group processes (such as involving conformity e.g. Moscovici *et al.* 1969) play a role in jury deliberation (see Chapter 4). The Stanford Prison Experiment, a key study in this book shows how group processes can lead to a breakdown of human decency in a simulated prison (Zimbardo 1973, see Chapter 5).

Additionally, much violence is partly the result of deficient social information processing. We will examine that in detail in Chapter 2, where criminal thinking patterns are discussed. It highlights that the social approach is not just about the direct effect that other people have on us. It also involves the way we think about our social environment and the motives of others. Miscalculations on that front form part of the explanation of crime.

It is important to stress that no one approach or explanation is always right. In general, psychological approaches are methods by which we can come to an understanding of criminal behaviour. They do not provide a complete picture on their own. Human behaviour is too complex to suggest that one way of looking at it is always the best way forward. When discussing the wide variety of criminal behaviours, we must be flexible and pragmatic. It is therefore best to regard these approaches as part of a toolkit that we can use in order to understand human behaviour (Eysenck 2000). Knowledge of these approaches is important, so that they can be brought to bear when required.

Activity

Steve was a difficult baby, and a hyperactive child. As a teenager he started smoking at an early age and taking alcohol and illegal drugs. He calls himself an 'addictive personality'. Other issues include a poor relationship with his father who frequently beat him and always put him down. He says he has always been closer to his friends, most of them also delinquent. His numeracy and literacy skills remain poor. His first case of violence that led to an arrest was when he assaulted a shop keeper because he thought he was given the incorrect change. He was mistaken.

Since then there have been numerous assaults, often further to disagreements and arguments. Steve is now 26, unemployed, with no history of secure employment. He lives on benefits and has lost contact with his parents. He is quite heavily drug and alcohol dependent. The crime for which Steve was arrested yesterday was an assault outside a pub. Heavily intoxicated, he bumped into someone, who pushed him off. A fight ensued in which Steve broke the victim's nose and cheekbone. The victim ended up in hospital requiring surgery and will not be able to work for several weeks.

Imagine that you are Steve's probation officer. You might be asked to write a report on Steve advising the Court on Steve's background and to suggest a suitable sentence. Discuss the following points. Refer back to the approaches in criminal psychology section in Chapter 1.

- What are the main underlying causes of Steve's violent behaviour?
- What are the specific circumstances that prompt his aggression?
- Are there ways in which this can be addressed?
- What punishment would be suitable?

Are we living in a crime society?

Modern societies are in the process of learning to live with millions of crimes per year. Consequently crime features heavily in the news, in television dramas, and in public discourse. Although to become a victim of a serious crime is actually a rare event, concern about crime shapes our everyday activities. Crime, in short, is part of the backdrop of our lives.

On any given day, there are plenty of crime stories in the news media. These often concern crimes of a violent or sexual nature. In addition, there are many news reports that suggest that the criminal justice system cannot cope. For instance, the

BBC reported that convictions for rape hit a record low in 2005. The number of rapes reported to the police is rising – but only 5.6 per cent of 11,766 reports in 2002 led to a rapist being convicted (BBC News 2005). At the same time however, we learn that prison figures have risen to record levels. Prisons are overcrowded and it is said that they are reaching breaking point.

News editors know that crime stories are among the best-read news items. The same is true of internet news sites and blogs. Through the media it does indeed seem as if crime is everywhere. But does that mean that we live in a crime society? In order to assess the state of crime in society we must firstly establish the rate of crime. In this chapter, we will discuss police statistics, victim surveys, self-report studies and observational data. We will discover that all methods of counting crime have their limitations and conclude that counting crime is in fact far from easy.

In addition, we must consider how the risk of falling victim to crime shapes our lives. We will look at research into fear of crime, and into the financial and emotional costs incurred because of crime. But we must also think about the many other ways in which crime carries meaning. On the one hand, crime is a worry, but on the other hand, talking and thinking about crime can be quite exciting. Even committing a crime, many a juvenile offender would attest, can be quite exhilarating. In Chapter 2 we will discuss psychological theories on why offenders commit crime and 'the thrill of it', is certainly a factor. Thus, to live in a 'crime society' means being aware of and being exposed to crime in a variety of ways. The remainder of this chapter will explore exactly how crime in its various manifestations affects our lives.

How much crime?

For decades, policymakers have attempted to measure the 'true' extent of crime. The true prevalence of offending behaviour is important to establish as it can serve as a benchmark. *Reliable* crime statistics allow us to gain a picture of crime as a whole and its fluctuations over time. That will help us decide whether crime policies are successful. In addition, crime statistics allow us to make comparisons between cities, areas, regions or whole countries. That is useful as we may want to investigate so-called low crime countries and assess what it is that makes their management of crime so successful.

Wandsworth Prison. One of London's (and Britain's) busiest prisons.
Photo courtesy of Francis Pakes.

Official statistics

In 2005/06, the police in England and Wales recorded over 5.5 million crimes. There were 765 homicides (which includes murders, manslaughters and infanticides, which is defined as the killing of a child younger than one-year-old). Some two out of three homicide victims are male, and four out of five known perpetrators were men. The weapons used most often for male and female victims are listed below in Table 1.1.

In 2005/06 the police in England and Wales recorded just over 1 million violent crimes and 14,449 reports of rape. Altogether, in 2005/06 over 62,000 sexual offences were recorded and some 645,000 burglaries.

Table 1.1 Homicide by method for male and female victims in 2005/06

	Male victims (%)	Female victims (%)
Sharp object	31	23
Hitting, kicking, etc.	18	8
Shooting	8	4
Blunt instrument	8	8
Poison/drugs	4	4
Explosives	4	12
Strangulation	4	16
Burning	4	4
Other	19	21

Source: Coleman *et al.* (2007).

Police recorded crime is currently falling but not to a large extent. It peaked around 2003/04. Over the course of the 20th century, recorded crime has risen enormously. Table 1.2 below shows rates of murder, violent crime, sexual crime and all recorded crime in 1900, 1910, 1920 and onwards. In 1900, the police in England and Wales recorded fewer than 80,000 crimes. That hardly compares to today with over 1 million instances of violence alone recorded by the police in 2005. Despite the massive rise, there are some offences that actually occur less frequently today than they once did. One of those is the offence of 'concealing child birth'. This probably reflects changing attitudes towards unmarried mothers and unplanned pregnancy.

Table 1.2   Officially recorded crime 1900–2005

	Homicide	Total violence	Total sex offences	All recorded offences
1900	312	1,908	1,582	77,934
1910	288	1,972	1,962	103,132
1920	313	1,546	3,070	100,827
1930	300	2,123	3,546	147,031
1940	288	2,424	4,626	305,114
1950	346	6,249	13,185	461,435
1960	288	15,759	19,937	743,713
1970	393	41,088	24,163	1,555,995
1980	620	97,246	21,107	2,688,235
1990	669	184,665	29,044	4,543,611
2000	850	600,922	37,311	5,170,843
2005	765	1,059,913	62,081	5,556,513

Source: Nicholas *et al.* 2006.

These figures paint a compelling picture. However, we must emphasise that police statistics are not proper indicators for the true extent of crime. We can therefore say that as a measurement tool they lack *validity*. There are a number of reasons for this.

Firstly, many victims do not report their crime to the police. Victims might for instance think that the crime they suffered is not serious enough, or that the police would not be able to help them. In addition, we must realise that within certain groups in society there are substantial levels of distrust towards the police. They might be less inclined to report victimisation than other groups. This might be the case for, for instance, prostitutes or individuals with a criminal record. Thus, confidence in the police is a factor that correlates with police reported crime (Newburn 2007).

In addition, people might not realise that they have become victims of a crime. They might assume that their mobile phone was lost, rather than stolen, for instance. Similarly, as crime definitions can be complex, victims might not realise that what happens to them is not just a nuisance, but is actually a criminal offence. For instance, a woman victim might simply not know that an ex-boyfriend who repeatedly harasses her might actually be committing the offence of stalking.

Court statistics suffer from the same drawbacks as police data.

Validity

A measurement's *validity* is determined by the extent to which it measures what it intends to. Police statistics only record crime reported to, or discovered by the police. But there is, in fact, a world of crime that never gets reported or even discovered. This can vary from intricate fraud scams, to petty theft, to serious sexual offending. Because of that, police statistics are a measurement of low validity to measure the 'true' rate of crime.

What is not reported to the police is most unlikely to come to the attention of the criminal courts. Thus, in summary, what the police, the Crown Prosecution Service and the criminal courts encounter, is only a subset of all crime. It is probably better to ask the public precisely about their experience of crime, and use that as a measure of how much crime actually occurs. That is exactly what the British Crime Survey sets out to do.

Ten million crimes: the British Crime Survey

The British Crime Survey (BCS) is conducted under auspices of the Home Office. It asks a representative national sample of people over 16 years of age living in private households about their experiences of crime and of the criminal justice system. It was first held in 1982 and was carried out every two years. Since 2001, the survey has been carried out continuously and its results reported annually. The 2005 measurement involved no less than 48,000 interviews. It formed the basis of a Home Office publication by Walker *et al.* (2006) called *Crime in England and Wales 2005/06*.

Based on these BCS data, Walker and colleagues estimate that in the year measured 10.9 million crimes had occurred against individuals over 16 years of age living in private households. The good news is that since 1995 there has been a reduction in crime of 44 per cent. Accordingly, the risk of becoming a victim of crime within a year has been reduced to 23 per cent (it was 40 per cent in 1995). That means that fewer than 1 in 4 people were the victim of a crime. Property crime (such as theft and burglary) accounts for over three quarters (77 per cent) of all crime.

These statistics suggest that society has become considerably safer since 1995. Unfortunately, many citizens do not feel that way. In the British Crime Survey, 63 per cent of respondents said that they thought crime had actually increased. Interestingly, the percentage of people who said that crime in their local area had increased is actually substantially lower, at 42 per cent. Readers of tabloid newspapers were twice as likely to say that crime had increased than broadsheet readers. Women were more likely to think the crime rate had increased 'a lot' (34 per cent of women and 25 per cent of men were of that opinion). In addition, older people were more likely than younger age groups to think that the crime rate had gone up. Finally, these impressions varied according to levels of education: 38 per cent of people who had no educational qualifications thought that crime in the country had risen compared with only 21 per cent of people with a university degree (Walker *et al.* 2006).

It is important to realise that according to self-report victimisation surveys, the rate of crime has decreased much further than when looking at police statistics. That is the picture of the last decade. The long term trend, however, is very different. If we compare crime rates from the 1960s with those of the 1990s, we see a massive increase. That indicates substantial social change. Thus, the crime picture of society in the days of our grandparents was very different from the one we see today. But many of us have been born into a 'ten million crime society', as that has been the state of affairs for about 20 years.

Despite the fact that the BCS is extensive and elaborate, it has its limitations and it is not without its critics. The box below outlines the areas where the BCS fails to obtain reliable figures on rates of crime. Due to these limitations, it has been argued by Jock Young that large scale victimisation surveys are no more than a *numbers game*. Counting crime is not the same as understanding the nature of crime. Young uses the term 'voodoo criminology' for such flawed endeavours (Young 2004).

Evaluate

The British Crime Survey: what it does not show

Over 40,000 people are interviewed for the BCS every year. It goes to great lengths to make sure that its sample is *representative* for the population in Britain. For that reason, it works with a sample of households throughout England and Wales. In every household, one person over 16 years of age is interviewed. On occasion, the BCS additionally includes a so-called booster sample of ethnic minorities to ensure that these minorities are properly represented. In order to encourage respondents to respond truthfully about sensitive matters, respondents can enter answers on sexual and domestic violence questions themselves on a laptop computer. All participants are ensured that their data will be handled anonymously and confidentially (Crowther 2007).

Despite all this, the BCS cannot provide a full and complete picture of crime. Firstly, it excludes certain groups of respondents:

- Under 16s;
- People not in private households, such as people in psychiatric institutions, probation hostels, and the homeless;
- Businesses.

In addition, the BCS is likely to under-represent crimes that do not necessarily come to the notice of citizens, or who might not think to mention it. These can include:

- Identity fraud;
- Internet fraud;
- Benefit fraud;
- Tax fraud;
- Traffic offences;
- Environmental crimes;
- Transnational crimes.

Thus, although the BCS might provide the most precise measurement of crime, it cannot provide a completely accurate state of affairs.

Other ways of counting crime: observational and self-report studies

With such criticisms in mind, researchers have developed other ways of counting crime. Some of these occur in settings not covered by large-scale victimisation surveys. Binder and McNiel conducted an observational study on a psychiatric hospital ward. Over a three-year period they documented 510 instances of violence against staff, mostly against nurses. They concluded that 'violent behaviour is a significant occupational hazard on acute inpatient units' (Binder and McNiel 1994: 245). Whittington and Wykes (1994) also looked at aggression by psychiatric in-patients against staff. They documented 63 instances of assaults by patients on staff. Eighty-six per cent of the assaults were immediately preceded by the assaulted nurse having delivered an aversive stimulus to the patient, such as giving an injection, or a refusal of a patient's request. Staff viewed many of these assaults not as crimes but as occupational hazards. Most nurses felt that such incidents are simply part of working in such environments.

Field studies like these might be the only way of establishing levels of crime in relatively 'closed' environments such as psychiatric hospital wards. That is not only relevant with regard to establishing the true extent of crime in society. It is also of interest because people in such settings are likely to interpret and manage violence differently. Therefore, they add a valuable dimension to crime research. Do note that these studies are not experimental but observational. As such, they can help identify the extent of crime, but struggle to provide insight into its causes.

Other survey measurements of crime focus on those younger than 16 years of age. The Home Office runs a survey specifically focused on youngsters, the Offending, Crime and Justice Survey (Wilson *et al.* 2006). In contrast to the British Crime Survey, it also asks about the respondents' own offending behaviour. We can therefore call the Offending, Crime and Justice Survey in part a *self-report* survey on crime.

In total 25 per cent of respondents revealed that they had committed an offence in the last 12 months. The most commonly reported offence categories were assault (committed by 16 per cent) and 'other thefts' (11 per cent). Four per cent of young people admitted to having carried a knife in the last 12 months. Seven per cent of all young people were classified as frequent offenders: they had committed six or more offences in the last 12 months. This seven per cent was responsible for the vast majority (83 per cent) of all offences measured in the survey (Wilson *et al.* 2006).

Looking at victimisation, just over a quarter (27 per cent) of young people had been the victim of personal crime in the last 12 months. The most common forms of victimisation were assault without injury (11 per cent) and other personal thefts (9 per cent). The majority of incidents against 10- to 15-year-olds happened at school, perpetrated by fellow pupils or friends. These incidents were mostly seen by the victims as 'something that happens' and 'wrong but not a crime' (Wilson *et al.* 2006).

The Offending, Crime and Justice Survey suffers from similar drawbacks as the British Crime Survey. It excludes certain groups, such as those in young offenders institutions, and those without fixed abode. Thus, the most serious and prolific offenders may well be excluded from the survey. In addition, there is the possibility that a *non-response bias* has occurred. That means that those who refused to take part may well differ from those who did: the non-responders may have lifestyles that are more chaotic and may be more hostile to people seen to be representing government. They are also more likely to have mental health problems, literacy weaknesses and social and verbal skills deficits. In addition, the survey, as does the BCS, relies on respondents understanding the questions and answering honestly, something that we perhaps might not take for granted in answering questions about offending behaviour.

Table 1.3. The main methods of establishing the rate of crime

Method	Main advantage	Main disadvantage
Police statistics	Reliable due to precise recording methodologies	Low validity as most crime is not reported
Crime victim surveys	Large representative sample, high validity and reliability	Certain groups are excluded, certain crimes likely to be excluded
Observational studies	High validity as observations are direct	Findings difficult to generalise to other settings
Self report studies	Representative sampling, high reliability	Issues of honesty (validity) and non response bias

Psychologist in profile

'Research methods are so important'

Dr Nicky Miller
Principal Analyst, Serious Crime Analysis Section
National Police Improvement Agency, Bramshill

I initially studied Applied Psychology and Sociology at Surrey University. Part of my course involved a placement during which I spent time with Hertfordshire Police and that is where I caught the bug! My fascination for psychology and policing set in there, and has stayed with me ever since.

I went on to do a PhD. It was in Investigative Psychology and involved the linguistic analysis of threatening letters. I was looking at ways in which to decide whether such threats are credible and likely to be carried out.

I worked on the Home Office's Organised Crime Research Programme for a number of years. My role was not that of a psychologist, but rather as an analyst and researcher. I did find that my psychology degree provided me with good knowledge on human behaviour and the research methods I learnt were absolutely invaluable. Research methods are so important. You need them to make sure that your findings are relevant and valid. As they might be used in crime analysis, you do not want poorly carried out research to invalidate your findings.

At the Home Office we looked at, among other things human trafficking and credit card fraud. These are relatively new forms of crime, and at the time there was not much good research on them, exactly how they are committed and by what sort of people. Our research was not so much policy oriented, but oriented towards practical applications. That has always excited me most.

Since a year and a half ago I work at the National Police Improvement Agency at Bramshill in Hampshire. I am a Principal Analyst at the Serious Crime Analysis Section. I continue to be involved with understanding serious offending, and at the moment we are looking into offences such as male rape and homosexual homicide. Psychology has provided me with useful knowledge on how to analyse and research such behaviours. That is very important to me. You have to understand the research process in order to understand the value of research findings. I do practical research in the field of criminal psychology, but it is not at all glamorous or exciting as some television programmes might suggest. Our aim is to provide the police with good knowledge on serious crime and the people responsible. That said, knowing that the research is actually being used, and can help in solving crime is very important to me. What I do on a daily basis might not be all that exciting, but the purpose it serves still is!

That said, respondents were asked, at the end of the survey if they answered all questions honestly, and 98 per cent said that they had (and the extent to which that answer was always honest is, of course, unknown).

Measuring antisocial behaviour

We saw earlier that despite a fall in crime, levels of worry about crime remain high. In addition, there is widespread concern regarding 'crime's little brother', antisocial behaviour. Antisocial behaviour is defined in the Criminal Justice Act 1998 as: 'behaviour that caused or was likely to cause harassment, alarm or distress to one or more persons not of the same household as himself'. Hatcher and Hollin explain that it can include 'using and selling drugs, harassment, graffiti, verbal abuse, damage to property, excessive noise, alcohol abuse, prostitution, intimidation, and criminal behaviour' (Hatcher and Hollin 2005: 166). That shows that criminal and antisocial behaviour are not entirely separate entities, but that their definitions overlap. Harradine *et al.* (2004) distinguish four types of antisocial behaviour. These are:

1 Misuse of public spaces, such as begging and public drunkenness;
2 Disregard for community and personal well-being. This includes noise, rowdy behaviour and hoax calls;
3 Acts against people, such as intimidation, name calling, racist remarks, etc.;
4 Environmental damage, such as litter and vandalism.

Antisocial behaviour is defined rather loosely. It can include any sort of behaviour that causes harassment, alarm or distress. That loose definition makes counting acts of antisocial behaviour even more difficult than counting instances of crime (Whitehead *et al.* 2003). However, in 2003 the Home Office's Antisocial Behaviour Unit organised a so-called 'day-count' of antisocial behaviour. They documented over 66,000 antisocial behaviours in one day in England and Wales (Home Office 2003). That is one every two seconds, and would amount to over 24 million acts of antisocial behaviour per year.

The BCS includes questions about respondents' experiences with
antisocial behaviour in their local area. One in six people say
that they experience a high level of antisocial behaviour in their
area. That is down four per cent from 2003. The table below
lists the eight types of antisocial behaviour most commonly
identified.

In order to combat antisocial behaviour, the Antisocial
Behaviour Act 2003 introduced Antisocial Behaviour Orders, or
ASBOs, which can be imposed by a judge on an individual. They
set limitations on a person's behaviour. ASBOs might prohibit
an individual to enter a certain area (such as a shopping centre),
or carry out certain behaviours (drink alcohol in public, for
instance). A breach of such an order can lead to imprisonment.

What is a crime? Definitions, understandings and labels

When we discussed the Offending, Crime and Justice Survey
for youngsters we noticed that respondents regularly mentioned
events that are in fact crimes, but not perceived as such. That
was particularly the case of incidents at school involving other
pupils. It is in fact quite possible for crime victims to feel that
what happened to them is actually not really a crime at all.
It is important to explore this further as it will help us think
about the nature of crime, and which behaviours we label as
criminal.

Table 1.4 Commonly identified antisocial behaviour

Percentage of people saying fairly/very big problem in their area	2002/03 (%)	2005/06 (%)
High level of antisocial behaviour generally	21	17
Abandoned or burnt out cars	25	10
Noisy neighbours/loud parties	10	10
People being drunk/rowdy in public places	23	24
People using or dealing drugs	32	27
Tenagers hanging around on the streets	32	32
Rubbish or litter lying around	33	30
Vandalism, graffiti or other damage to property	35	29

Source: Harradine *et al.* (2004).

Key study: Rape and sexual assault in the British Crime Survey

Rape and sexual assault of women: findings from the British Crime Survey

Aim
To assess the frequency of sexual victimisation and the views of victims.

Method
The data gathered come from the British Crime Survey (see main text). The BCS is a large random survey of private households, designed to give a count of crime that includes incidents not reported to the police. The questions on sexual victimisation were administered to women using a method of computerised self-completion. 'Rape' is defined in this report as 'forced to have sexual intercourse (vaginal or anal penetration)'.

Results
* Around 1 in 20 women (4.9 per cent) said they had been raped since age 16. About 1 in 10 women (9.7 per cent) said they had experienced some form of sexual victimisation (including rape) since age 16;
* Women aged 16 to 24 were more likely to say they had been sexually victimised in the last year than older women;
* Strangers were responsible for only 8 per cent of rapes reported to the survey;
* The police came to know about only 20 per cent of rapes;
* Less than two-thirds (60 per cent) of female rape victims were prepared to self-classify their experience as 'rape'.

Discussion
An important part of Myhill and Allen's research involves victims' own perceptions of what happened to them. Generally, only 60 per cent of rape victims classified what happened to them as a crime (Myhill and Allen 2002: 5). In addition to this, around a fifth (18 per cent) of women victimised by a 'date' considered the incident to be 'just something that happens' (Myhill and Allen 2002: 5). No more than one in five rapes was reported to the police. Myhill and Allen explain this as follows:

'These findings can be seen to provide further evidence to support the notion that the concept of 'rape' carries with it a specific set of meanings, assumptions and stereotypes. It may also be difficult for women raped by somebody they know, perhaps even somebody they liked or loved, to label this person a rapist'. (Myhill and Allen 2002: 5)

Knowledge of stereotypes helps us to understand why many victims who were raped by someone they know are reluctant to label their offenders as a 'rapist' or a 'sex offender'. They simply do not fit the stereotype.

Source: Myhill and Allen (2002).

Historical and cultural aspects

The labelling of crimes is dependent on historical and cultural factors. Nowhere is this clearer than in the area of drugs. Certain harmful and addictive substances are legal in the UK, but not necessarily elsewhere. Alcohol and nicotine are highly damaging, yet not illegal although licensing laws seek to restrict their use.

In addition criminal definitions change over time. In the US between 1920 and 1933 the manufacture, transport, and sale of alcohol was prohibited. The era is now known as the 'prohibition era'. In addition, there are many countries in which homosexuality or adultery are considered crimes. Thus, what is considered a crime changes over time and from one country to another.

Crime is a dynamic concept, and new developments produce new forms of crime. New crimes include publishing objectionable materials via the internet, and identity fraud (Wall 2007). Stalking is another example (see box). Stalking laws are only about a decade old. Much of the behaviour exhibited by stalkers (such as threatening behaviours) is criminal in its own right. However, not until recently has the essence of stalking, a patterned way to bring about fear in a victim, been defined as a specific form of crime.

Stalking: a 21st century crime

You might be forgiven for thinking that stalking is something that just happens to celebrities. Some devoted fans go to great lengths to meet their idol, and sometimes seem deluded enough to think that these stars actually secretly love them. To be fair, such events do happen, but not very often. The case of Madonna however, is a case in point. Obsessed fan Robert Dewey Hoskins managed to gain entry into Madonna's Los Angeles home carrying a wooden heart that read, 'Love to my wife Madonna'. He managed to stay inside her property for several minutes. He even had a swim in the pool. He eventually was shot by a member of Madonna's security team and charged with stalking the singer. Eight months later, Hoskins was convicted and sentenced to ten years imprisonment. Madonna appeared in court in Los Angeles to testify, an experience that made her 'sick to her stomach' (MacFarlane 1997). Such deluded individuals are sometimes found to suffer from *erotomania*.

However, stalking mostly happens to ordinary people, and most victims are women. Sheridan and Davies define stalking as 'a set of actions which, taken as a whole, amount to harassment or intimidation directed at one individual by another' (Sheridan and Davies 2001: 134). The 2001 BCS found that 19 per cent of women and 12 per cent of men reported having been victimised this way. Within the survey stalking was defined as 'a course of conduct involving two or more events of harassment causing fear, alarm or distress, of three types: phone calls or letters; loitering outside home or work; or damaged property' (Walby and Allen 2004: 5).

Budd *et al.* (2000) found young women to be particularly at risk, as 16.8 per cent of women aged 16 to 19 and 7.8 per cent of those aged 20 to 24 recalled being subject to persistent and unwanted attention during the previous year. Risks were high among women who were single, students, living in privately rented accommodation, living in a flat or maisonette, and living in a lower income household. Thus, whereas media reports rather focus on stalking as a crime to particularly haunt the rich and famous, the data from the BCS show that in fact the opposite is true (Pakes and Winstone 2007).

Another disturbing finding is that stalking is not just awkward behaviour by passionate but inadequate admirers. A good majority of offenders know their victim and often know them rather well. Only 12% were complete strangers but almost half (48%) were either ex-husband, ex-wife or former boyfriend or girlfriend. Most other stalkers are acquaintances of various kinds, often neighbours but also regularly fellow students or clients in some kind of professional context. Many stalkers engage in damaging behaviour, prompting Brewster to emphasise that it is control, rather than love or a desire to be together that motivates most stalkers:

An objective observer might not understand the rationale for stalking (…). In trying to make sense of stalking behaviour, it is clear that the desire to control the former partner is a great, if not the most important, motivating factor. (Brewster 2003: 216)

Crime as a social construction

Crimes could be defined as harmful acts committed by in-dividuals who are, to a certain degree, culpable, i.e. blame-worthy. That is the traditional *consensus* view of crime. This definition suggests that we all agree that certain behaviours are wrong, and it is these that should be labelled as criminal.

However, there are opposing viewpoints (Dwyer 2001). There is the view that we should think about crime in the context of society. Societies can be unequal and unfair. That inequality, so the reasoning goes, creates a moral duty to violate some of its codes. Robin Hood, after all is a folk hero who stole from the rich to give to the poor. Despite engaging in theft and robbery, we think of Robin Hood as 'one of the good guys'. If the distribution of goods in society is unfair, then perhaps theft can be justified.

A further consideration is that much harmful behaviour is in fact not defined as criminal. With increased concern over climate change and potentially increased shortages of energy, water and food, we should perhaps criminalise wasteful behaviour. Perhaps in future leaving the tap on or unnecessary car journeys will be crimes.

A 'no consensus' view on crime: the case of 'honour killings'

The organisation Human Rights Watch (2001) defines 'honour killings' as follows:

Honour crimes are acts of violence, usually murder, committed by male family members against female family members, who are held to have brought dishonour upon the family. A woman can be targeted by (individuals within) her family for a variety of reasons, including: refusing to enter into an arranged marriage, being the victim of a sexual assault, seeking a divorce — even from an abusive husband — or (allegedly) committing adultery. The mere perception that a woman has behaved in a way that 'dishonours' her family is sufficient to trigger an attack on her life. (Human Rights Watch 2001: 4)

The United Nations (2004) estimate that some 5,000 honour killings occur worldwide every year. Welchman and Hossain (2006) stress that the conditions in which such honour killings occur have a lot to do with poverty and the position of women in society. They are less well explained by religion, as honour killings occur among Muslims, Christians in West Africa, and Hindi and Sikh communities in India. They mostly tend to occur in poor and rural areas.

Honour killings challenge the consensus view on crime: if we cannot even agree that murder is always wrong, there is little basis to assume that what constitutes a crime is something that we can always agree on.

In summary, we cannot say that crimes are only those behaviours that everyone agrees are wrong. The labelling of crime is a complex social and political process. In some instances, such as violent and sexual offences, our crime categories tend to be reflections of the consensus model of crime. But bear in mind that even in the case of murder, different cultural conceptions may exist. The case of honour killings is a pertinent example (see box), and perhaps terrorism is another example: abhorred by many, but justifiable according to others. Most people will agree on crimes most of the time, but do not forget that there is always an element of subjectivity and arbitrariness involved.

Think

Can you think of three types of behaviour that at present are not crimes, but that you think should be criminal? Make sure that these behaviours are common, harmful in some respect, and that those who carry out these acts are culpable.

Counting crime versus understanding crime

Crime affects us in many ways. One of these effects is our continuous efforts to avoid becoming a victim. We lock our doors and keep valuables in a safe place. We do not give out personal information to strangers. We are mindful in providing information on the Internet. We keep our PIN code safe and we are careful outside after dark. Crime affects society: we spend billions of pounds on police, courts and prisons, but also on CCTV cameras, private security officers, alarm systems and self-defence courses.

Despite the high costs, many of us are fascinated by crime. Crime novels abound in the bestseller lists and television police and detective series capture huge and committed audiences. Ingenious crimes intrigue us, whilst serial killers provide a source of great fascination. 'Crime talk' serves a wider function. Crime stories, particularly involving child victims help us teach our children on how to be safe, particularly regarding 'stranger danger'. Before mass media, fairytales and folk stories had that function. Today, it is crime stories that achieve that purpose. Crime stories serve a 'norm affirming function'. That means that crime reports help us to talk about what is right and wrong, and about how to be safe.

Finally, we must be wary of seeking to understand crime solely from the perspective of offenders being 'driven' to crime. Katz (1988) has argued that crime can be seductive, and that the rewards of crime can be both highly tangible, and very direct.

Young argued that we must understand the 'phenomenology of crime': 'its adrenaline, its pleasure and panic, its excitement, and its anger, rage and humiliation, its desperation and its edgework' (Young 2004: 13). That perspective is required when we think about criminal subcultures such as youth gangs.

Understanding fear of crime

Are you worried about crime? Most people are at some point in their lives and in particular in certain situations. When you are walking around after dark in an area you do not know very well, and you hear shouting and running footsteps, you are bound to be wary. We call that a *state* of fear. It is of relatively short duration, and comes and goes when the situation in which it is experienced changes. Most people would argue that this is quite a rational response. After all, many situations we enter carry an element of risk.

Fear of crime as a *trait* involves a generalised fear that people feel for prolonged periods of time. It is not tied to specific situations but rather is more like a 'force from within'. People who possess such a trait perceive the world differently. They are more likely to regard neutral situations as frightening. As a result they might be significantly more moved to take precautions against crime or to restrict their behaviour in order to avoid becoming a victim (Pakes and Winstone 2007).

Fear of crime can be either a social or a personal worry. A social worry would involve the judgement that crime in society is getting out of hand. But that does not have to be accompanied by a fear for your own personal safety (Ferraro 1995). We define fear of crime as a personal concern about becoming a victim. Personal fear of crime is a commodity that is unevenly distributed in society. Some groups of people are much more fearful than others.

Female fears

Women have been frequently found to be more fearful than men (Stanko 1992). The 2001 BCS uncovered that women are more worried than men about being burgled, mugged and physically attacked. Women are most disproportionately at risk in the area of sexual offending, where they are eleven times more likely to become a victim, than men (Tjaden and Thoennes 1998). It has been suggested that their vulnerability towards sex offending makes it no more than realistic for women to be more fearful of crime generally and to adjust their daily behaviour to a degree in light of that. That said the relation between gender and fear of crime is not always straightforward, as age plays a part too. Older women tend to be more fearful than older men. Young women are also particularly worried but middle-aged women less so. Ferraro suggests that women of different ages are afraid of different things. Increased fear of crime amongst young women is a lot to do with sexual offences. Elderly women instead are more concerned about any sort of contact crime such as robbery or mugging due to their increased physical vulnerability (Ferraro 1995).

Urban unease

People who live in urban areas report more fear than those in rural areas (British Crime Survey 2001). However, crime is a relatively urban phenomenon, so again, this may in fact be a rational response. Type of neighbourhood impacts on the levels of fear reported by residents as well. Graffiti, drugs and disorder enhance feelings of insecurity and fear whereas good relationships with neighbours serve to reduce such sentiments. Also possibly related is the finding that those with lower incomes are more fearful. Those who are unemployed are twice as likely to be afraid than those in employment. However, do note that such relationships are correlational. That does not mean that the relationships are causal: fear of crime is a variable that is difficult to manipulate directly and the same is true for the factors that affect it. We therefore have to resort to correlational designs.

The fear of crime paradox

Many criminologists have compared fear of crime with actual risk of becoming a victim. A paradox, which is a seemingly inconsistent state of affairs, is often noted; those who are most fearful are least likely to become a victim, whereas those who do not seem to be too bothered about victimisation are in fact the group most vulnerable: the latter group comprises outgoing young males.

Stanko (1992) found that although men are more likely to be victims of crime, women report levels of fear that are three times as high. Scott argues that a key factor in understanding this disparity lies in the fear of sexual violence. In particular young women report most fear of sexual crimes. As we saw earlier that young women are also most likely to be victimised in this way, we cannot say that that fear is somehow irrational or an over-reaction.

An important aspect of fear of crime research is to what extent a person's worry about crime influences their behaviour. Young (no date) argues that this can go as far as a self-imposed 'curfew', with women simply not leaving the house after dark.

A survey of 13,000 Canadian women found that most women were fairly or very worried out at night (Scott 2003). Walking alone in their neighbourhood at night worried 61 per cent; 75 per cent were very or fairly worried about using public transport at night, and 81.3 per cent were afraid to use car parking garages at night. What is worse, perhaps, is that 39 per cent also report being fairly or very worried about being at home alone at night.

It clearly shows that fear of crime is something that many if not most women have been forced to learn to live with. Many tend to avoid certain situations and if they do go out at night, they do so with trepidation. Many routinely take safety precautions. Past experience of fear for the so-called stranger leads to the most changes in behaviour:

> Receiving obscene phone calls, or having been followed by an unknown male, and/or receiving unwanted attention from unknown males were all strongly and significantly predictive of higher levels of fear in all situations. What this suggests is that experience with male strangers plays a stronger formative role in fear production in the lives of women than how old they are, whether they are single, what their financial resources may be, and to a lesser extent what educational achievements they may have made over their lives. (Scott 2003: 211).

Think

Would becoming a victim change your behaviour?
Consider the following three types of crime and consider ways in which it might change your behaviour. What would you change?

1 An assault in a pub late at night;
2 An assault on the street near where you live in broad daylight;
3 A burglary while you were asleep.

Thus, although we must mention the fear of crime paradox, we must also appreciate that fear of crime brought about by 'stranger danger', may well be an entirely appropriate response.

In addition, those who display most avoidance behaviour remain most fearful: thus, whilst their avoidance of fearful situations might put them less at risk, they are no less worried. This reminds us of the work of Mowrer (1947) on phobias. He proposed a two-stage model: the acquisition of phobias occurs via *classical conditioning*, but they are maintained via *operant conditioning*, in particular via avoidance behaviour. The reward is the relief from the anxiety associated with, for instance, going out after dark.

Activity

Fear of crime: design a questionnaire

Imagine you want to establish whether people who are physically fit are less fearful of crime. That might be the case because they might feel better able to confront an attacker. It might also be that people who are physically fit might have higher self-esteem and confidence. That might reduce fear as well.

Questionnaires need to be short. Apart from asking about age and questions to establish levels of fitness, you have five questions to ask about fear of crime.

In a small group, design these five questions on fear of crime. Consider the following:

First decide:
- Are you addressing fear of crime as a state or as a trait?
- Do you include cognitive, emotional and/or behavioural criteria?
- Do you look at experience of victimisation?

Then decide on the nature and type of questions, such as whether to use open/closed question, or Likert scales: for instance, five point scales to measure attitudes.

In summary, fear of crime is often rational, when we take into account the risk of victimisation, the damage to the individual that crime will do, and the fact that people project the state of their local environment onto their fear of crime. Those elements together make it imperative that we should not only seek to reduce crime, but that in order to improve the quality of people's lives, we should strive to reduce fear of crime in tandem.

Key study: Crime and fear of crime on holiday

Fear of crime among British holidaymakers

Aim
The study considers how fear and worry varies among holidaymakers according to their experience of crime.

Method
Participants
Questionnaires were submitted to subscribers of *HolidayWhich?* magazine. Indicative of the magazine's readership, respondents were relatively old (modal age 55) and predominantly male. Respondents were also more affluent than the general population and were also more likely to have a burglar alarm, and therefore do not constitute a *representative* sample.

Procedure
A total of 1,100 questionnaires were distributed to readers of which 47 per cent were returned.

Results
Percentage rate of victimisation on holiday compared to British Crime Survey's estimated victimisation rate in UK

	% rate of victimisation on holiday	% estimated rate of victimisation (according to BCS)
Theft of motor vehicle	2.04	.1
Theft from motor vehicle	2.04	.48
Burglary	4.67	.32*
Violence	2.14	.34

*includes attempted burglary.

The results show that people suffer much higher incidents of victimisation on holiday than they otherwise would at home. Further, the authors state that tourists are more likely to be the victim of a crime compared to the local residents.

In addition, the authors also asked tourists how safe they felt or would have felt walking alone after dark. Only 7 per cent reported feeling unsafe on holiday compared to 31 per cent at home. Similarly, 62 per cent of people expressed worry about being burgled at home and 47 per cent of being mugged. Yet, in this study's sample, only 8 per cent and 9 per cent respectively of holidaymakers expressed these feelings of concern.

Discussion
Unlike victimisation at home, on holiday actual crime exceeds fear of crime. Perhaps when on holiday, we are not worried enough.

Source: Mawby *et al.* (2002).

Police detention. Could you be a custody officer?
Photo courtesy of Jan Brayley (Hampshire Constabulary).

Chapter 2

The causes of crime

The question of 'why?'

We often ask ourselves what is wrong with people who commit crimes. Why would an individual vandalise a bus stop? Why does an elderly patient lash out at the nurse who takes care of her? Our fascination with crime often concerns the apparently inexplicable: the dark forces that drive a serial killer, or the thrill of senseless violence. Certain types of crime simply defy comprehension.

On the other hand we must not forget that often the reasons for crime are quite straightforward. Theft and fraud can provide material gain. Sexual offences can provide sexual gratification. Violence can release negative feelings or establish dominance. Graffiti can be both a crime and a way of self-expression. The gains that crime can bring are often very clear, but the risks they carry equally so.

Art or crime? Graffiti is an expressive crime: the crime is its own reward.

Photo courtesy of Francis Pakes.

We can distinguish two types of motivations for crime: crimes can be instrumental or expressive. *Instrumental crimes* are a means to an end. When an offender steals goods to buy drugs to feed a habit that is instrumental crime. It is not about the crime *per se*, but about the profit that it brings. *Expressive crimes*, on the other hand, are their own motivation. Graffiti, as we see above can be an expressive crime, whereas hate crimes and vandalism are often expressive as well: the offender does not expect any further gain from that offence, the crime itself is the sole motivation.

Activity

Look at a newspaper and find a number of crime stories. Are the crimes discussed instrumental or expressive? Can they be both?

Think about:
Do newspapers report all crimes or some offences more than others? What crime stories are more likely to create a media interest than others?

Whatever their motivation, it is well established that some people with certain characteristics are more likely to commit offences than others. Identifying such factors and looking at ways of influencing them is an important area of criminal psychology. In this section we will look at a number of such factors. The first are biological and genetic factors. Subsequently we examine whether personality factors can have a bearing on crime. After that we discuss social learning and subsequently we look at the role of moral reasoning in understanding delinquent behaviour. From there we look at cognitive distortions which are thinking patterns that criminals are more likely to exhibit. After discussing these thinking patterns we more specifically look at aggression and violence.

Biological and genetic explanations

The skull measurers

It is tempting to assume that those who commit offences are fundamentally different to the rest of the population. Such a categorisation would provide a clear understanding of our social world. In this perspective, most people are assumed to be honest and law-abiding citizens. In contrast then, there would

Psychologist in profile

'Many fire-setters have personal or mental health difficulties'

Dr Katarina Fritzon
Chartered Forensic Psychologist
Bond University, Australia

'I began my career as a forensic psychologist in the UK, but I recently emigrated to Australia. I completed an undergraduate degree in Psychology at Aberdeen University, in Scotland. This awakened my interest in the criminal mind, and I then went to on to do a Masters that was run by Professor David Canter, who was one of the pioneers of 'offender profiling' in the UK. My subsequent PhD was on the psychology of fire-setting. Many fire-setters have personal or mental health difficulties, and these might be evidenced in the way they commit their offences.

I then started working as a lecturer at Surrey University. I also worked in treatment of offenders, at Broadmoor hospital and the Dene Medium Secure Hospital in West Sussex with patients who had been convicted for arson. It was around this time that myself and my husband visited Australia on holiday. We decided shortly after that we would like to emigrate and soon after we moved to the Gold Coast and I took up a position as Assistant Professor in Forensic Psychology at Bond University. Since coming here, I have continued working in the area of arson treatment, and recently completed a 20-week treatment programme with an individual at a prison in New South Wales who had been responsible for a very large bush fire. I very much enjoy working as a forensic psychologist and have moved quite a long way from my original roots as an Investigative Psychologist, both academically and geographically.'

be a small minority of people who are mean and dangerous, and they are that way because there is something wrong with them. This is, however, a stereotype. Stereotypical views of offenders are commonplace, but often inaccurate.

The reality of crime is not so simple as to be captured in simple stereotypes. The vast majority of young men admit to having on occasion broken the law and a good majority of all men have been in trouble with the police at one time or another (Farrington 1995). That rather suggests that crime is something that most of us engage in at some point or another. It therefore does not make sense to assume that all offending behaviour is due to some kind of biological or genetic deficit.

Yet there once was, in the nineteenth century, a tradition of studies that were based on the very assumption that criminals are different. Cesare Lombroso was the quintessential advocate of this type of research. He was a nineteenth century Italian physician who argued that there are four types of delinquents. There are so-called born criminals, or atavists, insane criminals, occasional criminals and passion criminals. Most criminals commit crimes because they are inferior to well developed and adjusted human beings. That inferiority is both biological and genetic, in Lombroso's view. Born criminals have not evolved quite as far as other people. Because of that, they are more equipped to live in the wild rather than in civilised society. These evolutionary misfits can be recognised by their physical features. According to Lombroso, if you know what to look for, you can easily tell criminals apart. The box below lists the characteristics of born criminals.

Features of born criminals, according to Lombroso (1876):

- Unusually short or tall height;
- Small head, but large face;
- Small and sloping forehead;
- Receding hairline;
- Wrinkles on forehead and face;
- Large sinus cavities or bumpy face;
- Large, protruding ears;
- Bumps on head, particularly the 'destructiveness centre' behind ear;
- Protuberances (bumps) on head;
- High cheek bones;
- Bushy eyebrows;
- Large eye sockets;
- Deep, beady eyes;
- Beaked nose (up or down) or flat nose;
- Strong jaw line;
- Fleshy lips, but thin upper lip;
- Mighty incisors, abnormal teeth;
- Small or weak chin;
- Thin neck;
- Sloping shoulders, but large chest;
- Long arms;
- Pointy, webby, stubby fingers or toes;
- Tattoos on body.

Examine the features listed in the box above. Note that Lombroso considered an area behind the ear as the 'destructiveness centre'. The notion that bumps on the head are indicative of certain traits comes from an approach that is called *phrenology*. It has long since been discredited, as has Lombroso's work.

Brain research

We reject the notion of criminals as inferior or degenerated. But that does not mean that there might not be subtle biological influences that, in conjunction with other factors can have a bearing on offending behaviour. In recent years, technology has afforded us to look closer into patterns of brain activity, a much more relevant variable than skull shape. This can be performed via Electro Encephalographic measures (EEGs) measuring the electronic activity of the brain, and via Positron Emission Tomography (PET scans) with which highly localised brain activity can be measured. PET scans allow us to assess whether certain areas of the brain function differently in serious criminals than others. The study carried out by Raine and colleagues is an excellent example of this type of research as it shows that subtle differences in brain functioning can be demonstrated (see key study).

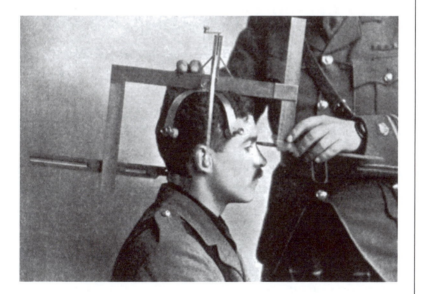

The skull measurers. In the nineteenth century skull measuring was performed to assess mental faculties. This type of research has long since been discredited.

Key study: The brains of murderers

Brain abnormalities in murderers indicated by positron emission tomography

Aim

To assess whether murderers (found not guilty by reason of insanity) might have specific localised brain dysfunctions.

Method

Participants

Forty-one murderers who pleaded not guilty by reason of insanity (which means that they committed the crime but were judged to be 'insane' at the time) to a murder charge in California, US. They were 39 men and two women, average age 34 years. They suffered from a variety of mental health problems, including head injury or brain damage (n=23), schizophrenia (n=6); and paranoid personality disorder (n=2). Their brain scans were compared to a matched control group of 39 men and two women with an average age of 31. They were matched on gender, age and on schizophrenia, but not on brain injury.

Procedure

All participants underwent a continuous PET scan that lasted 32 minutes during which the participants carried out a task.

Results

The group of murderers had lower activity in the prefrontal cortex area of the brain, as evidenced by lower rates of metabolism in those areas. This was found for both the left and the right hemisphere. In addition, murderers' brain activity was characterised by asymmetrical activation, with the left hemisphere less active than the right. There were other areas in which murderers had lower brain activity, such as the corpus callosum although their activity in the occipital part of the brain was higher. Due to the small sample size the level of statistical significance was set at 10 per cent.

Discussion

Subtle differences in brain functioning for murderers were found. They occur in the prefrontal cortex, in an area called the limbic system that governs the expression of emotion. Other areas affected included the so-called *behavioural inhibition system*. That said, it does not mean the brain dysfunction is guaranteed to produce violence, or murder: 'these findings cannot be taken to demonstrate that violence is determined by biology alone: clearly social, psychological, cultural and situational factors also play important roles' (Raine *et al.* 505.). In addition the design of the study did not allow Raine *et al.* to establish whether these dysfunctions are the result of nature, nurture or both.

Source: Raine et al. (1997).

Twin studies

The reasoning behind twin studies is straightforward: identical twins are assumed to have identical genes. Thus, any differences between the two would be the influence of the environment. If identical twins are more similar in their offending behaviour than other siblings, that would provide a degree of evidence for a genetic influence. It was indeed found by Christiansen (1977) that identical (monozychotic) twins resemble each other closer in criminal behaviour than non-identical (fraternal or dizychotic) twins. Based on his analysis of the criminal records of no less than 3,586 pairs of twins, he found that if one identical twin had a criminal record, there was a 35 per cent chance that the other twin did too. For non-identical twins, this figure was only 12 per cent.

However, we cannot simple ascribe Christiansen's findings to the influences of genes. We can expect that people are likely to treat a pair of identical twins the same. The twins may grow up together, go to the same school, have the same friends and enjoy the same social activities. As a result it is not just that their genes are identical but so to a large extent is their environment. We can therefore not disentangle any genetic influence from environmental factors.

Nature vs nurture

Remember that we cannot reduce the causes of criminal behaviour to simply either nature or nurture. The effect of genes on behaviour is highly indirect. In addition, the effects of genetic make-up can only manifest itself via its interaction with the environment. Claridge and Davis (2003) argue that 'it is unlikely that there are genes, or sets of genes for impulsivity, the preference for gay relationships, religiosity, anxiety or even serious mental disorders'. Thus, if there is an influence of genes, it is likely to be small and indirect.

Adoption studies

A better way of establishing the influence of genes is via adoption studies. Such studies look at children who have been adopted shortly after birth and we establish whether their behaviour resembles that of their natural parents or that of their adoptive parents. If the former is the case, that is evidence for the influence of genes. The latter is evidence for the importance of the environment in shaping delinquent behaviour. Mednick et al. (1984) looked at 14,427 adopted children in Denmark. It was found that when both adoptive and biological parents had a criminal record 24.5 per cent of sons became criminal as well. With only a criminal biological parent, the figure was 20 per cent. With only an adoptive parent with a criminal conviction 14.7 per cent of sons acquired a criminal record themselves and only 13.5 per cent had a criminal conviction even if none of their adoptive or their biological parents had one. Blackburn suggests that this implies a 'modest genetic contribution to crime' (Blackburn 1993: 141).

The Dutch gene disorder

We must stress that by itself our genetic make up does not constitute a major cause of crime. However, this is not to discount the famous finding by Brunner and colleagues who studied a Dutch family in which a gene defect was genetically transmitted through the family (Brunner *et al.* 1993). In this large family only the men were affected by the faulty gene. They showed various problem behaviours including increased aggression. The aggression was displayed in a variety of ways, but was usually impulsive and not calculated. Some women in the family did carry the gene but it did not show any effect. Brunner's study highlights that genetic defects, in rare cases, can produce increased impulsive aggression (Brunner *et al.* 1993). Although we can say that genes generally do not explain much in terms of criminal behaviour we cannot categorically state that they do not matter (Pakes and Winstone 2007).

Table 2.1 The percentage of adopted sons with a criminal conviction as a function of criminality by biological and adoptive parents

Criminal conviction parents	Sons with criminal convictions (%)
Both biological and adoptive	24.5
Biological parent only	20.0
Adoptive parent only	14.7
Neither	13.5

Source: Mednick *et al.* 1984.

Twin studies are still being conducted at present. They have moved beyond establishing whether criminals are born or made. It is generally accepted that it is not a case of 'either–or'. Instead, such studies examine how genetic and environment influences interact to produce, in some cases, criminal behaviour. Moffitt and colleagues run a project that is called the Twins Early Development Study. The group follows a set of 1,116 twins, and their families in the UK (Plomin and Asbury 2005).

The research group has identified various factors that can make problem behaviour more likely. Problem behaviours include bullying, aggression and cruelty to animals. These are often precursors to juvenile delinquency. Some of these factors have a genetic component, such as hyperactivity. But they do not *cause* crime by themselves. However, they are risk factors. If the hyperactive or highly impulsive child is also exposed to harsh or erratic parenting, or lives in a chaotic home where alcohol or drug abuse occurs, then criminal behaviour in later life is more likely (Jaffee *et al.* 2005).

Determinism

The study by Jaffee *et al.* utilises the biological approach. That approach can be both reductionist and deterministic. Reductionism refers to the notion that psychological explanations can be reduced to biological explanations. Determinism is the philosophical position that human behaviour is not brought about by free will but determined by other factors.

Personality factors

It has been suggested that criminals are more likely to be thrill seekers, that they have less tolerance for frustration and that they are more impulsive than non-criminals. Hans Eysenck (1977) argued that some of these personality traits might have a genetic basis.

A key factor in his work is the difference between *introversion* and *extroversion*. Introverts are people who enjoy their own company. They tend to be quiet, reserved and think before they act. In contrast, extroverts are individuals that enjoy large gatherings of people. They tend to be chatty, gregarious and impulsive. According to Eysenck (1977) these attributes are more than a personal style or preference. Instead, they tell us something fundamental about our brain. Eysenck argued that extroverts are under-aroused. They need stimulation. In addition, Eysenck thought that extroverts are less likely to be affected by negative outcomes of their behaviour, such as punishment. If something goes wrong and the game is up, extroverts are more likely to shrug their shoulders at the disapproval of others. Introverts on the other hand will not deal with negative feedback or punishment so casually. They will take it to heart.

Eysenck emphasised the role of such general personality traits in understanding why some people are more likely to commit crime, if only for the thrill of it, than others. There is no doubt that the commission of certain offences can be exciting adventures. The incentive for joyriding is often so explained. In addition, if extroverts are less sensitive to punishment, that might offer further explanation why these people are less likely to refrain from offending.

Eysenck's personality dimensions are *psychoticism, extroversion* and *neuroticism*. These dimensions consist of a good number of constituent factors that we will not discuss here in detail (for that, see Eysenck and Gudjonsson 1989). High scores on psychoticism

Early risk factors for later delinquency

Individual factors
- Early antisocial behaviour (physical aggression, biting, cruelty to animals);
- Poor cognitive development;
- Low intelligence;
- Hyperactivity.

Family factors
- Maltreatment;
- Family violence;
- Parental psychopathology;
- Familial antisocial behaviours;
- Teenage parenthood.

School and community factors
- Poor academic performance;
- Low academic aspirations;
- Living in a poor family;
- Disorganised neighbourhoods;
- Delinquent peer groups.

Source: Loeber and Farrington (2001).

Extroversion and introversion

Extroversion	Introversion
adventurous	quiet
assertive	reserved
frank	shy
sociable	unsociable
impulsive	considered

Source: Eysenck and Gudjonsson (1979).

relate to vulnerability to mental illness, whereas very low scores on this trait indicate conscientiousness and agreeableness. Extroversion we already described whereas the trait neuroticism is to do with negative mental states. Those who score high on neuroticism are more likely to frequently feel anxious, depressed and isolated. Prison inmates score higher on psychoticism and extroversion as well as on neuroticism (Eysenck and Gudjonsson 1979).

That finding should not surprise us. We can see the argument that extroversion, in particular impulsivity can explain certain types of offending. On the other hand it is important to realise that such scores obtained by Eysenck and Gudjonsson might be a reflection of the inmates' current prison experience, rather than of their offending behaviour that got them into prison in the first place. We know that serious mental illness is not uncommon behind prison walls. Prison is certainly not a good place to be for inmates with a vulnerability to such illnesses (Singleton *et al.* 1998). Blackburn therefore concludes that Eysenck's theory of criminality is 'not well supported' (Blackburn 1993: 127), despite the fact that correlates between criminal behaviour and personality traits have been obtained. That reminds us of the fact that correlation and causation are not the same thing.

More recently Eysenck's personality constructs have been subsumed into a five factor model of personality (McCrae and Costa 1999). These five factors are openness to experience, conscientiousness, extroversion, agreeableness and neuroticism (OCEAN). There is little doubt that serious or prolific delinquents score higher on some of these factors than others (Miller and Lynam 2001).

Evaluate

Why do prison inmates score high on extroversion, neuroticism and psychoticism?

Such findings are sometimes seen to demonstrate that those who offend have a different personality. However, we must remember that:

- Their answers on the questionnaires can be influenced by *demand characteristics*, that is, they might be affected by what they think the experimenter is expecting to find.
- Their answers can be influenced by concerns of self-presentation, and their desire to come across as tough.
- The prison experience might have brought out a part of their personality that was not dominant before.
- Prison may have brought about problems of depression and anxiety and they may have affected their scores on some of Eysenck's personality dimensions.

Thus we cannot conclude from such studies that criminals differ in personality from non-criminals, or that certain personality traits cause criminal behaviour.

Based on a meta-analysis in which they reviewed over 20 studies, Miller and Lynam (2001) were able to identify several traits that were strongly associated with antisocial behaviour. Individuals who commit crimes and other antisocial acts are more likely to be hostile, self-centered, spiteful, jealous and indifferent to others. In addition, they tend to lack ambition, motivation and perseverance, and they have difficulty controlling their impulses. Finally they are more likely to hold non-traditional and unconventional values and beliefs. Interestingly, they did not find extroversion to be a significant factor.

Personality

Personality aspects are relatively stable and enduring aspects of individuals which distinguish them from others making them unique, but which at the same time allow people to be compared with each other (Gross 2005). But bear in mind that some personality traits are more stable than others. McCrae *et al.* (2000) found that 'openness to experience' is a trait that decreases over the lifespan whereas most people score higher on 'agreeableness' and 'conscientiousness' as they get older. Does a life span perspective on personality help in explaining why most people stop committing offences when they become adults?

Gottfredson and Hirschi (1990) argued that the essential difference between criminals and non-criminals is their degree of self-control. They argue that the question should not be why certain individuals commit crimes. Given the benefits of crime and the often low chances of getting caught, why do we not all break the law all the time? They stated that self-control is the essential difference between those who do commit crimes and those who do not.

The area of personality and crime is not quite crystallised. That is not least because the very area of personality research is vibrant with new personality structures recently proposed. There is no doubt that there are some personality factors at work in the area of crime. A certain temperament with a certain attitude to life and towards other people no doubt facilitates offending. That said it is difficult to pinpoint exactly which personality traits or even how many different traits there are that pertain to offending behaviour.

Moral reasoning

Most crimes involve a decision to commit them. That invites the question whether criminals make different decisions than others or whether their reasoning styles or capabilities are in one way or another to blame. This section will look at whether offenders have a different moral outlook to the rest of the population and whether their moral reasoning levels or styles are distinctive.

Psychometrics

Psychometrics refers to the science of measuring human qualities such as personality. The psychometric approach seeks to compare individuals by assigned numerical quantities to their traits, such as personality or intelligence. The strength of this approach is its scientific approach and replicable results. However, a number of disadvantages have been identified as well. Such psychometric tests may not be valid or reliable. They might contain *cultural biases*. In addition, a value assigned to an individual (such as highly neurotic, or of low intelligence) can serve as a negative label. That is important as it is often assumed that once established, these scores typify us over the life course, and that may well be inaccurate. Therefore, a score on a psychometric test may even become a *self-fulfilling prophecy*. Others therefore say that it is better to assume that we are all unique and that our strengths and weaknesses should not be reduced to numerical scores. That, in fact, represents the *ideographic approach* to personality (Gross 2005).

Kohlberg's stages of moral reasoning

Moral reasoning is not all that easy to measure. It is part of the essence of moral reasoning that 'better' or 'worse' is difficult to establish. The field's most well-known researcher, Kohlberg has been credited with a breakthrough: he disentangled the *outcome* of moral reasoning from the reasoning *process*. Simply put, he was not so much interested in the decisions people make, but how they do it. He asked participants to discuss so-called moral dilemmas. A moral dilemma is, you could say, a no-win situation in which whatever you choose, you inevitably have to violate a rule or a moral principle. A famous example of a moral dilemma that Kohlberg used is Heinz's dilemma (see box).

Kohlberg initially studied the moral reasoning of 72 boys from Chicago, aged between ten and 16 years old by asking them about Heinz's dilemma and similar dilemmas. It was a longitudinal study; the boys were reassessed every three years to establish how their reasoning had changed (Colby *et al.* 1983; Kohlberg 1984).

Heinz's dilemma

A woman was dying from a rare kind of cancer. There was one type of medication that the doctors thought might save her. It was a form of radium that a chemist in the same town had recently discovered. The drug was expensive to make but the chemist charged ten times what the medication had cost him to make. He paid £200 for the radium and charged £2,000 for a small dose of the drug. The sick woman's husband, Heinz, went to everyone he knew to borrow the money, but he could only get together about £1,000, which was half of what the drug cost. He told the chemist that his wife was dying and asked him to sell it cheaper or let him pay later. But, the chemist said, 'no, I discovered the drug and I'm going to make money from it.' So Heinz got desperate and considered breaking into the man's shop to steal the drug for his wife.

1 Should Heinz steal the medication?
2 Suppose the person dying is not his wife but a stranger. Should Heinz steal the drug for a stranger?
3 Is it important for people to do everything they can to save another's life?
4 Is it against the law for Heinz to steal? Does that make it morally wrong?

Adapted from Kohlberg (1984).

Inspired by the developmental stages proposed by Piaget, Kohlberg postulated six stages of moral development. It is assumed that individuals acquire the ability to reason at higher levels when they mature. The six stages comprise three levels of moral reasoning. At the *preconventional level* rules are external to the self. They are simply imposed by adults and morality is shaped by the consequences of breaking or following these rules. At the *conventional level*, rules are to an extent internalised. We

Kohlberg's stages of morality

Level 1 preconventional morality
Stage 1 punishment and obedience
Moral behaviour is no more than the avoidance of punishment. A person reasoning at this level will not do certain things simply because if caught, they are in trouble.
Stage 2 instrumental and egocentric
What is right and wrong is determined by assessing rewards and risks. A person reasoning at this level is still essentially egocentric.

Level 2 conventional morality
Stage 3 interpersonal concordance
Moral behaviour is guided by the extent to which it meets approval from others. People reasoning at this level are likely to adopt the values of their friends or family unthinkingly as their own.
Stage 4 maintaining social order
Reasoning at stage 4 involves acknowledging the importance of the 'common good' and laws and rules are seen to be vital to an ordered society.

Level 3 postconventional morality
Stage 5 social contract
Morality is no longer mirrored on friends, family or even society. Instead, the person reasoning at this level realises that laws are not set in stone and that there can be overriding principles that on occasion justify breaking the law.
Stage 6 universal ethical principles
The person has acquired a highly developed and personal set of beliefs that guides their moral reasoning. It is realised that society's rules are to an extent arbitrary and bound by current values. The person instead relies on universal values, and they may clash with what is perceived to be right and wrong by any given society at any given point in time.

Source: Palmer (2005).

realise that rules are there for a reason and that most of the time we are better off taking them into account. At the *postconventional level*, morality has evolved into something more sophisticated. It is informed by human rights and ethical principles.

The three levels consist of two stages each, see above. Kohlberg postulated that immature individuals are only able to reason at the lower levels. In addition, the more mature individual is not only able to reason at a higher level, but will also have a strong preference for it. Finally, we tend to be able to follow the reason that is one stage higher than our own level of reasoning. Although we do not tend to apply it, it does make sense to us. On the other hand, the reasoning of more than one level upwards does not make sense to the individual: small children will not understand the meaning of a social contract, and slightly older people will not grasp how ideas right and wrong can be shaped by universal ethical principles (Palmer 2003).

Evaluating Kohlberg's theory

The assumption of moral progression, i.e. that individuals reason at a higher level when they mature is validated by Kohlberg's research. Colby *et al.* (1983) indeed found that reasoning does seem to go through a number of distinct stages. Children under nine years of age tend to reason at the preconventional level and adolescents and adults typically reason at the conventional level (Ashkar and Kenny 2007). Kohlberg did acknowledge that not everyone will reach Stage 6 or even Stage 5.

Kohlberg's theory has been criticised for containing a gender bias. Recall that Kohlberg's participants were all boys. Do women think differently about moral issues? Johnston (1988) has argued that there is no difference in competence which is the focus of Kohlberg's research but there might be differences in preference. Women might be more inclined to discuss moral dilemmas in terms of care, rather than framing them as issues of justice (Haste *et al.* 1998).

In addition, there have been concerns of a cultural bias in Kohlberg's work. Kohlberg places great emphasis on justice as a key moral orientation. It has been argued that that is mostly a Western, perhaps even an American pre-occupation. Ethics and morals in parts of Eastern Asia are informed by family loyalty, whereas Hindus in India involve religious considerations much more strongly in their decision making. Finally, specifically to Heinz's dilemma in which the value of preserving life is at stake, it was found that where US participants were inclined to place the highest value on maintaining life *per se*, Japanese individuals prioritised the quality of life. In their view, life was not always worth saving if the quality of life was very poor (Iwasa 1992).

Psychologist in profile

'Mentally disordered offenders can be difficult to work with. But that's a challenge I enjoy'

Dr Chris Ainsworth
Consultant Clinical Psychologist
St. James's Hospital, Portsmouth

'I work with patients who are both mentally ill or have a personality disorder and have committed a crime, or are perceived to be a risk to themselves or others.

I initially studied Applied Psychology at Liverpool John Moores University. I then worked for two years as a psychological assistant after which I gained a place on the Clinical Doctorate Programme at Southampton University. That is a three-year programme with a number of placements in various mental health settings. My dissertation was on eating disorders, but I became increasingly interested in forensic work.

I currently work in St. James's Hospital in Portsmouth on a low secure forensic unit. That is a hospital ward, but with a reasonable level of security. The doors are locked! We have 13 beds for mental health patients who have committed a crime, are suspected of having committed a crime, or who are at risk of becoming violent or dangerous. They often suffer from a psychotic disorder or a personality disorder. Added to that are often problems with substance misuse.

To give an example, I recently worked with a sex offender with a history of indecent exposure but who committed two counts of rape a few years later. A key part of his cognitive behavioural treatment programme involved working on his anger. In addition, we did a lot of offence-specific work to tackle psychosexual issues.

I also work with offenders in the community and in the local prison as well. When a prisoner displays symptoms of mental illness, I might advise on whether that individual should be transferred out of prison to a hospital setting. But there is often a shortage of places, or long delays.

Mentally disordered offenders can be difficult to work with. But that is a challenge I enjoy. Some people think that you cannot really treat these people but you can get results. You can improve a person's health, their skills and improve their quality of life. Most importantly, you can reduce their risk of reoffending. And that is good for all of us.'

Furthermore, high level moral reasoning relies on good verbal skills. You need to be able to 'talk the talk' and express yourself cogently in order to demonstrate postconventional moral reasoning capabilities. It refers to a key issue with Kohlberg's research: just because individuals *talk* high-level morals, does that mean that they always *behave* in a moral manner as well? At first sight we would think that that's unlikely, after all, talk is cheap.

Ashkar and Kenny argue that criminals tend to reason at the preconventional level, instead of at the conventional level which is more typical for adults. That is indeed what Palmer and Hollin (1998, 2000) found. This finding is sometimes explained in terms of 'arrested development'. Whereas other youngsters mature and develop their moral reasoning, the reasoning of delinquents remains egocentric and that might help explain their behaviour.

Aleixo and Norris (2000) set out to establish whether it was personality, moral reasoning or both that explained offending in young offenders. They administered the revised Eysenck personality questionnaire (Eysenck *et al.* 1985) to establish levels of psychoticism, neuroticism and extroversion/introversion, and the so-called socio-moral reflection measure (Gibbs and Widaman 1982) to establish levels of moral reasoning. They also asked their participants about their offending behaviour and various personal details. Their participants were 101 juvenile delinquents (aged between 16 and 22) at a young offenders' institution. All volunteered.

The young offenders scored higher than average on extroversion, neuroticism and psychoticism and lower than average on the moral reasoning measure. There was substantial reasoning at Level 3, but also a significant number of Stage 2 argumentation. That is in line with expectations. However, the link to crime was intriguing. Psychoticism was correlated with certain crimes but not with others. It did relate to theft but not with crimes against the person such as violence. Extroversion in contrast was related to crimes against the person. More surprising perhaps is the fact that levels of moral reasoning did not relate to offending behaviour at all. Instead they found a correlation between number of siblings and offending behaviour: the larger the family, the more likely it is that offending behaviour occurs. Aleixo and Norris therefore conclude that 'support was found for the theory of H.J. Eysenck, but no support was found for that of Kohlberg' (Aleixo and Norris 2000: 621). That is in contrast to the work of Palmer and Hollin and it suggests that other factors have been at play in producing these results.

Given the criticisms levelled against Kohlberg's six-stage model of moral development it is no surprise that other researchers

Key study: delinquents' moral reasoning

The interrelations of socio-moral reasoning, perceptions of own parenting and attributions of intent with self-reported delinquency

Aim
To establish whether young offenders' moral reasoning is at a lower le0vel than non-offenders'.

Method
Participants
Ninety-seven convicted male, young offenders between 13 and 21 years (mean 18.18 years) and 77 male non-offenders aged between 12 and 24 years (mean 17.41 years). Non-offenders came from skilled-manual or intermediate non-manual backgrounds, while the offenders were from unemployed or unskilled-manual backgrounds. The offences committed by the offender sample were burglary, car theft and joyriding, robbery and assault.

Procedure
The researchers administered the following questionnaires:
- *Socio-moral reasoning.* The socio-moral reflection measure – short form involves 11 questions probing respondents' moral reasoning.
- *Perceptions of own parenting.* This involves 23 questions incorporating factors of rejection, emotional warmth and over-protection.
- *Attribution of intent.* Consists of 12 questions involving social situations that young people might find themselves in. Participants have to say whether the intention displayed in the situation is pro-social, hostile or ambiguous (see example below).
- *Self-report delinquency.* Records the nature of offences committed in the past year as well as the frequency of the offences from once a year to two or three times a day.

Results
- The researchers found significantly less advanced moral development among the delinquents.
- Offenders showed a greater hostile attribution bias in ambiguous situations and less correct attributions of pro-social intent.
- Perceptions of paternal rejection were found to be higher among the offender than the non-offender sample. Perceived parental rejection was also associated with a high hostile attribution style in both offenders and non-offenders.

Discussion
Palmer and Hollin (2000) establish a statistical relation between levels of moral reasoning and self-report delinquency. However, that does not mean that there is a straightforward causal relationship. The findings highlight the 'complex interactions' between the environment (such as parenting) and socio-cognitive processes (such as attribution of intent).

Source: Palmer and Hollin (2000).

have proposed more recent models. An often cited example is from Gibbs (2003) which is attractive for two reasons. Firstly it consists of no more than four stages. The lower two stages reflect immature moral reasoning and the higher two involve mature moral reasoning. It also takes into account the issue of gender preference in moral reasoning and the recognised role of empathy in reaching moral judgment. Gibbs's framework is summarised in the box below.

Activity

Interviewing and surveying criminals?
Palmer and Hollin among others, base many of their findings on questionnaire data from convicted criminals.
    In a group, come up with at least three reasons why that is a good way of gaining insight into crime, and three reasons why we should view such data with suspicion.

Cognitive distortions

Cognitive distortions are the result of inadequate thinking patterns. These thinking patterns may lead offenders to develop incorrect ideas regarding offending behaviour and victims. This is a shift in perspective as the research on moral reasoning looks at the level of reasoning, but not at the actual content or outcome of the reasoning process. In contrast, a focus on cognitive distortions suggests that the actual content of these cognitive distortions matters most.

Gibbs' four stages of moral reasoning

Immature moral reasoning
Stage 1 unilateral and physicalistic
Reasoning refers to authority figures and the immediate physical consequences of behaviour.

Stage 2 exchanging and instrumental
Reasoning reflects a basic understanding of social interaction, but typically restricted to cost-benefit deals, with the benefits to the individual of prime importance.

Mature moral reasoning
Stage 3 mutual and prosocial
Reasoning is underpinned by an understanding of interpersonal relationships and the norms and expectations associated with these. There is evidence of empathy and social perspective taking, and the influence of the person's conscience.

To link cognitive distortions to moral reasoning we have
to look at Kohlberg's Level 2. At this level, individuals are
guided strictly by behaviourist principles and are unable and
unwilling to place themselves in other people's shoes. Palmer
(2005) calls this the *primary cognitive distortion*, the egocentric
bias. Individuals with that bias are less able to consider the
effects of their actions on other people and instead place
emphasis on their own needs and desires.

In addition there are three *secondary cognitive distortions*. They
serve to justify behaviours that harm others by putting their
own interests first. The main secondary cognitive distortion is
the so-called *hostile attribution bias*. It refers to the tendency to
interpret ambiguous events as hostile to oneself. Imagine that
you're walking into a classroom and someone bumps into you
from behind. Why did they do that? You might be inclined to
assume that it was an accident, or that it probably is a classmate
who is just 'messing around'. Those attributions are pro-social.
Should you be inclined to assume that someone bumped into
you on purpose because they were picking a fight that would
be a hostile attribution.

Palmer and Hollin (2000) established the extent to which
young offenders display the hostile attribution bias. They gave
delinquents short scenarios and asked why the protagonist
would behave the way they did: to be nice, to be mean or
not sure why. The scenarios could be pro-social (they were
being nice), anti-social (they actually were mean or horrible)
or ambiguous (based on the information given, you could not
properly decide what their intentions were). The researchers
found that juvenile delinquents were slightly more likely to
rate ambiguous scenarios as hostile. That demonstrates that, to
some extent, a hostile attribution bias was present.

It is easy to imagine that a hostile attribution bias will
enhance the chance of certain encounters ending in violence.
If you are convinced that the person who spills your drink did
that on purpose you would be more inclined to respond in a
hostile fashion. Should they take offence with your reaction
the situation can easily escalate. The hostile attribution bias

might explain why certain situations are more likely to explode particularly when two people who both exhibit this bias would interact with each other.

Homeless in Toronto. Homelessness correlates with both offending behaviour and with becoming a victim.
Photo courtesy of Commissioner Machiel Roerink.

The second cognitive distortion is that of *excessively blaming others and external causes*. When individuals hurt others the cause of that behaviour is laid at the feet of others: they were asking for it, or should not have been doing what they were doing in the first place. This is another error of attribution.

The third distortion is the *minimalisation of the consequences of their actions*. That allows individuals to feel less guilt or remorse as if what they did was not all that bad. A burglar might argue that many victims would have insurance to cover material losses, so that burglary is not all that bad a crime. Such cognitive distortions can lower the threshold for criminal behaviour.

Have you got an attribution bias?
Consider the following two scenarios, from the attribution of intent questionnaire that Palmer and Hollin (2000) used.

'You're sitting at home watching TV one night. Your parents have gone out, so you're alone. There's a knock at the door. When you answer it there is a policeman standing there, who asks to speak to you.'

Does the policeman do this:

a) to be nice?
b) to be mean or horrible?
c) not sure why?

'You've just had your hair cut in a new style, but feel a bit unsure about how it suits you. As you walk into the classroom the next morning, a couple of people are whispering and giggling in the corner, although you're not sure what about.'

Do they do this:

a) to be nice?
b) to be mean?
c) not sure why?

Both scenarios are ambiguous: we do not know for sure why the police officer came round or why your classmates were giggling. However, juvenile offenders are somewhat more likely to say that they did this to be mean, than non-offending youngsters. Would you?

Attribution

The attribution process is the process by which we seek to identify causes for human behaviour, including our own (Gross 2005). Offenders are somewhat more likely to attribute their behaviours to the behaviour of others and to circumstances.

The causes of aggression and violence

Violent crime is a quintessential form of offending. The effects of victimisation can be devastating. Apart from physical injury, many victims suffer psychologically for a prolonged period of time. There is no doubt that violence is a most serious issue and one that has concerned criminal psychology for decades.

According to statistics derived from the British Crime Survey (BCS) (Nicholas *et al.* 2005) in 2004/05 the total number of violent offences in England and Wales was 2,412,000. These include:

- 401,000 incidents of domestic violence;
- 828,000 incidents where the offender was an acquaintance;
- 836,000 incidents where the offender was a stranger;
- 347,000 incidents of mugging.

Violent crime has fallen by 43 per cent since its peak in 1995 and has remained relatively stable since 2000 (Nicholas *et al.* 2005).

Thinking about violence

In thinking about violence, we must consider people, places, causes and consequences. Much psychological research relates to people: who becomes violent? But we must consider the 'where' of violence as well. There are settings that are associated with violence, such as certain pubs or clubs, or sporting events. But do not forget that many people are subjected to violence outside such 'high risk' settings. Most violence is domestic violence, and occurs between people who know each other intimately. In addition, workplace violence is an issue that is of growing concern.

It is a sad state of affairs that schools cannot be assumed to be safe havens. Figures from the BCS (Budd 1999) suggest that 3.2 per cent of teachers in primary schools and 4.2 per cent of teachers in secondary schools are victims of violence. Pupils and their parents are the two main sources of violence (Budd 1999). Katz *et al.* (2001) collected questionnaire and interview data from over 7,000 respondents aged between 13 and 18 years. The findings of the three data sets suggest that more than half of all children had been bullied and more than one in ten had been severely victimised (Katz *et al.* 2001).

Violence is not confined to certain places. That is an uncomfortable truth. It does mean that we cannot protect ourselves from violence by simply staying away from these areas. Violence might come to you instead. Knowing about the reality of aggression and violence is an essential part of criminal psychology. But it also is important from a perspective of being safe.

Defining aggression

Before discussing psychological research into violence, we need to talk about definitions. Definitions are the lens through which we look at the world. We all have a sense of what aggression or violence is. But if we define aggression in a certain way that might exclude behaviours that intuitively seem to be aggressive, regardless. Such a definition might be deemed to be too narrow. Conversely, we might define aggression very widely, but that might have the result that we need to look at behaviours that we do not feel justify the label aggression. Definitions need to be just right.

In the area of aggression and violence, definitions matter. We cannot begin to measure the extent of aggression and violence if we haven't agreed exactly what behaviours constitute aggression and which ones do not.

A good definition:

- Makes sense intuitively;
- Is clear and concise;
- Covers all behaviour that matters and excludes all others.

Definitions of aggression and violence tend to involve three components. The first is the actual act. Aggression and violence require some kind of observable behaviour. The second is the intention of the person who carries out the aggressive act. And thirdly, the effect on the victim is taken into account. Remember that definitions have a purpose. For instance, if a researcher wants to demonstrate how widespread violence is, it makes sense to 'define it down' and to include all minor acts. If, on the other hand, the intention is to show that violence is not a big problem, you define it up, and the prevalence will seemingly be lower. For the purposes of this chapter, we follow Berkowitz's (1993) definition that aggression is behaviour performed with the intention of harming someone.

Aggression as a drive

A superficial examination of aggression in animals might lead us to believe that being combative is beneficial. Male animals tend to fight over scarce resources. That can be food or drink, but also access to female mating partners. Sometimes the resource at stake is simply space. Indeed, male dominance behaviour is often associated with territoriality. To control a territory will secure resources for the animal and their offspring. A further advantage of the establishment of territories with boundaries is that it actually avoids aggression. When personal space is well defined, intrusions and confrontations are less likely to occur.

What is aggression?

A rugby player who carries out a legitimate tackle?	Yes/Possibly/No
A football player who commits a foul?	Yes/Possibly/No
A dissatisfied customer who grabs a shopkeeper by the collar?	Yes/Possibly/No
An angry executive who calls an employee a 'wally'?	Yes/Possibly/No
A four-year-old girl who snatches a toy out of her sister's hands?	Yes/Possibly/No
A car driver who makes a rude gesture to a crossing pedestrian?	Yes/Possibly/No

What is violence?

A rugby player who carries out an illegitimate tackle?	Yes/Possibly/No
A teacher ripping up a pupil's written assignment?	Yes/Possibly/No
A home owner slamming the door in the face of a sales person?	Yes/Possibly/No
A person making a racist remark to a taxi driver?	Yes/Possibly/No
A person staring at another in order to intimidate them?	Yes/Possibly/No
A patient who spits at a nurse in his face?	Yes/Possibly/No
A school pupil systematically ostracised by other pupils?	Yes/Possibly/No

Aggression

Aggression is behaviour performed with the intention of harming someone.

Therein lies an important lesson: animal behaviour is more precisely geared towards avoiding aggression. After all, violence can be highly costly. Red deer stags lock horns in order to establish dominance, but it is like fighting with gloves: the locking of the horns minimises the risk of injury. Chimpanzees have extensive rituals for intimidation, but usually avoid the physical fight. Aggression is ritualised and therefore contained (Gleitman 2003).

Lorenz (1966) looked at violence in relation to establishing dominance. He argued that the species would benefit from aggression if the result is that the stronger and healthier male specimens would be more likely to mate. His approach was decidedly biological: he felt that his research into animal aggression could be generalised to humans.

Frustration and aggression

Dollard *et al.* (1939) also state that aggression is an innate response but postulate that what triggers it is frustration and frustration only: 'aggression is always a consequence of frustration and contrariwise ... the existence of frustration always leads to some form of aggression'. The term 'always' should be viewed with suspicion. There are not many laws in psychology that are universal to the extent that they always apply.

The reasoning behind the so-called frustration–aggression hypothesis is straightforward. We all seek to achieve certain goals. When those goals are blocked, frustration occurs because the expected positive reinforcement is not achieved. Thus, there is a strong behaviourist undertone in Dollard's view on aggression.

Barker *et al.* (1941) showed that when children were shown an attractive set of toys but were not allowed to play with them, subsequent play was characterised by aggression against these toys. It seems a clear example of the aggression–frustration hypothesis at work.

Evaluate

Frustration and aggression: evaluating the link
Dollard *et al.* state that frustration always causes aggression and that aggression is always the result of frustration. Both parts of the statement have been challenged.

Miller suggested that frustration can lead to different responses, such as withdrawal and hopelessness. Alternatively, goal blockage might lead to more positive responses than frustration: we might just try harder.

Furthermore, whether we become aggressive will depend on our interpretation of why and how our goal was not achieved. If other people purposely frustrate us we are more likely to have our frustration lead to aggression than otherwise. That means that frustration is not a sufficient condition for aggression.

Finally, frustration is not a necessary condition either: violence can easily occur without it. Think, for instance about so-called *happy slapping*, where it seems that violence occurs for fun, and not as the result of frustration. Thus, although the link between frustration and aggression intuitively makes sense, it is far from complete as an explanation.

Excitation transfer

Zillman's excitation transfer theory provides some of the missing pieces that were identified after evaluating the frustration-aggression theory. In Zillman's experiments (Bryant and Zillman 1979; Zillman *et al.* 1972) participants are subjected to a (mild) provocation to which they cannot retaliate. In addition, these unfortunate participants had to endure a stimulus that heightens arousal, such as loud noise or physical exercise. Increased arousal did produce increased aggression but only if there also was provocation. When an individual has been provoked, increased bodily activity does increase the chance of violent behaviour. Zillman's findings augment Berkowitz's model as it is not only negative emotions that cause the body to physically prepare for violence. Positive energy can do the same thing.

Excitation transfer helps us to gain a fuller understanding of football hooliganism. We can understand that the fans of a losing team would be frustrated. That frustration may prompt violence. But what about violence initiated by followers of a winning team? Excitation transfer may be the answer. These supporters are excited and in a heightened state of arousal. It will then only require provocation for violence to occur.

Cognitive neoassociation

Berkowitz (1993) has further extended the frustration–aggression hypothesis. He called it the *cognitive neoassocation* theory. A key feature in this theory is *negative affect*. Negative affect refers to feelings, memories, and notions of both anger and fear. Negative affect is associated with increased arousal, either to fight or flight. That is the biological element in Berkowitz's framework. But the usage of the term 'cognitive' is significant. Berkowitz argues that cognition plays a major role in understanding aggression.

Negative affect changes our perception and interpretation of subsequent events. Thus, subsequent interactions are more likely to be perceived as frustrating or hostile. For example, when there is negative affect, warm weather is more likely to be perceived as oppressive rather than pleasant. Similarly, a delayed train is not just 'one of those things', but something that is really annoying. Negative affect also facilitates memories of other unpleasant events, and violent responses to situations are also more likely to occur to the individual. In short, negative affect facilitates angry thoughts, memories and associations. One seemingly innocent factor that can bring about negative affect is in fact, heat.

The idea that heat does affect us is what the so-called heat hypothesis postulates (Anderson 2001). In a real-life study,

Kenrick and MacFarlane (1986) found that aggressive use of the car horn increased on hot days, but only for drivers in cars without air conditioning, in the US state of Arizona. Anderson *et al.* (2000) estimate that a 2° Fahrenheit (just over 1° Celcius) increase in temperature accounts for an increase in the US murder rate by 9 per 100,000.

The cognitive neoassociation theory does predict that violence can be a self-fulfilling prophecy. Some people are more likely than others to seek situations in which conflict and frustration

Hot under the collar: researching the effect of heat on violence

Numerous studies have established a relation between high temperature and violence (Anderson 2001). However, we must realise that establishing such a correlation is not the same as establishing a causal relationship.

Studies into heat and violence are usually either *field studies* (that compare fluctuations in temperature with fluctuations in recorded in violence) or *experimental studies*. Both have their limitations. A number of factors need to be considered.

Field studies are unable to control for *confounding variables*. These include for instance the fact that during hot weather, more people might be spending time outside. That might increase the propensity for violent encounters. Hot summer evenings might also be conducive to excessive drinking. Thus, we cannot separate the effect of heat *per se* from the effect of changes in activity due to hot weather. Heat can lead to traffic jams (towards the beach and theme parks, for instance) and heat might particularly occur during summer holidays when people have more free time. Interestingly in the US, the heat hypothesis would suggest that murder rates in the hotter South must be higher than the cooler North. After controlling for other variables (of a socio-economic and cultural nature) it was indeed found that heat was a significant factor: hot cities experience more murders (Anderson 2001).

Experimental studies into heat and violence are subject to a lack of *ecological validity*. It is very difficult in laboratory settings to bring about violent behaviour due to obvious ethical and practical concerns. Anderson reports that laboratory studies in which heat was artificially induced quite often fail to demonstrate any link between heat and aggression. It probably is a case of *demand characteristics*, with participants assuming that the heat is there for a reason and therefore fail to respond naively to the situation. That said, when other measures are taken into account, such as feelings of hostility and endorsement of aggressive attitudes, it has been found that heat does tend to increase those.

is more likely to occur. So-called Type A individuals are more likely to shape their environment in this way. That in turn can bring about a habitual preference for aggressive 'solutions' to frustrating situations. That might serve to alienate them from peers and co-workers, which in turn can be frustrating, to which they respond in their usual confrontational manner. It might become a cycle out of which there seems to be no escape.

Aggressive modelling

Berkowitz's theory is, you might say, situational. It seeks to explain why aggression occurs in certain situations and it highlights the fact that events and situations may contain the seeds for violence. But how is aggression learnt in the first place?

The researcher to champion the importance of social learning in understanding aggression is Bandura (see key study). His so-called 'Bobo-doll' study is a classic in psychology.

Bandura's contribution to psychology is profound. Bandura has shown that the acquisition of aggression into a child's behavioural repertoire is not difficult. We do not need to delve deeply into the souls of disturbed individuals to find violence's causes. Instead, everyday situations contain part of the answer.

Type A Personality

Type A personality (Friedman and Rosenman 1974) is usually discussed in relation to stress and stress-related illnesses. But the construct has a link to aggression as well. Type A individuals are more prone to heart disease and are frequently competitive, impatient, get easily frustrated by others and confrontational. You would expect individuals with Type A personality to be highly successful in a professional environment. On the other hand, you can imagine that road rage or aggression towards others fits this type as well.

Bandura's Bobo-doll study demonstrated that young children, in particular boys, can be quite easily brought into a situation and frame of mind to produce aggressive behaviour. McGuire (2004) expanded on this, and specifically looked at why certain children are seemingly much more aggressive than others. He framed his findings in terms of social information processing. That is a cognitive approach to understanding aggression and violence. If your social information processing skills are poor,

Key study: Punching an inflatable doll

Transmission of aggression through imitation of aggressive models

Aim
To establish whether exposure to an aggressive adult model would reproduce imitative aggressive acts in young children.

Method
Participants
Participants were 36 boys and 36 girls aged between 37 and 69 months (mean 52 months) enrolled at Stanford University nursery.

Procedure
The children observed either an aggressive adult model or a non-aggressive model. These models were either the same or the opposite gender. The control group had no exposure to an adult model. Initially, the children were brought into the experimental room and the adult (the model) was invited to join them. Here, they played with potato prints and stickers.

The experimenter then escorted the model to the opposite corner which contained a small table and chair, a tinker toy set, a mallet and a 5-foot inflated Bobo-doll. The experimenter explained that these toys were for the adult to play with and then left the room.

For the children in the non-aggressive condition, the model assembled the tinker toys in a quiet subdued manner ignoring the Bobo-doll. In the aggressive condition the model most of the time (of the ten minutes) aggressed towards the doll.

Then, all the children had to be exposed to 'mild aggression arousal'. This was achieved by allowing the children to play with some highly attractive toys. But as soon as they were settled, the toys were taken away from them telling them that these toys had been reserved for other children.

Each child spent 20 minutes in this room with various aggressive and non-aggressive toys and was observed through a one-way mirror.

Results
Children in the aggression condition reproduced more physical and verbal aggressive behaviour towards the Bobo-doll. Boys produced more physical and verbal aggression than girls when exposed to a male model. By contrast, girls exposed to a female model performed more verbal aggressive acts than boys exposed to the female model. This interaction (gender of the child with gender of the model) failed to reach statistical significance but Bandura et al. still call it a considerable effect.

	Aggressive condition	
Number of aggressive acts	Male adult model	Female adullt model
Imitative physical aggressive		
Male children	25.8	12.4
Female children	7.2	5.5
Imitative verbal aggression		
Male children	12.7	4.3
Female children	2.0	13.7

Adapted from Bandura et al. (1961).

Discussion
Aggressive behaviour can be learnt by imitation. When the model is male his behaviour has the most powerful influence. These findings have relevance for our thinking towards both exposure to violence that children might have, but also on the role of gender stereotypes and violent behaviour.

Source: Bandura et al. (1961).

many situations are bewildering not to mention frightening. Most of the time, we have no difficulty in making sense of the situations that we are in. But you are probably able to recall situations that were confusing or embarrassing. That may well be caused because your social information processing let you down. That is often evidenced by seemingly inexplicable happenings. Why is John walking away? Is he angry or upset or did I miss something? Why is everybody laughing? Are they laughing at me? Confusion like this is likely to be the result of glitches in social information processing. Feelings of social inadequacy can be highly frustrating and that alone might make aggression more likely.

Violence and television

Few household items can be said to be more 'everyday' than television sets. At present, the average Briton watches television for about 3.5 hours a day (Ofcom 2006). The average daily time spent doing sports, in contrast, is about ten minutes. Television can be a source of entertainment, and a way of gaining knowledge. In 2005, 73 per cent of people said that they use the television news to gain knowledge of current events, as opposed to only 11 per cent who said that newspapers were their main source of information (Ofcom 2006).

Worry about the negative effects of television is almost as old as television itself. Stories of its harmful effect are publicised on a regular basis. The *Daily Telegraph*, under the

McGuire (2004) summarises that aggressive children:

- Encode fewer social cues;
- Encode less cues initially;
- Rely more on internal schemas;
- Selectively attend to aggressive cues;
- Generate fewer potential solutions;
- Select action-oriented rather than reflexive solutions;
- Manifest an egocentric perspective;
- Manifest a hostile attribution bias.

headline 'TV toddlers "become aggressive"', recently detailed US research that shows that toddlers who watch a lot of TV have shorter attention spans and display more aggressive behaviour (Womack 2007).

Violence on TV and its impact on viewers is one of the most vibrant research areas in criminal psychology. Huesmann and colleagues have conducted a longitudinal study in which they followed 557 children growing up in the Chicago area in the US (Huesmann *et al.* 2003). They assessed the television viewing habits of children aged six to ten and, years later, examined their levels of aggression as adults.

Huesmann *et al.* distinguish short-term effects from long-term effects. Short-term effects can be described as 'acting out' or imitation (Huesmann 1998). When people watch a violent movie, they might be inclined to act this out immediately afterwards, an effect similar to children playing football outside immediately after having seen football on TV.

Long-term effects are more complex to establish, as there are many potentially confounding factors. Nevertheless a number of findings have emerged. Firstly, there is evidence of an effect of television watching *per se*. The more television youngsters watch, the more likely they are to be aggressive as young adults. This effect is stronger for those who prefer violent programmes, who judge the violence in these programmes to be more realistic, and the ones who identified with the aggressive characters (Huesmann 1998).

Huesmann and colleagues also found that men who were high TV-violence watchers as children were significantly more likely to behave aggressively to their partners and to have responded to an insult with aggression. These men were three times more likely to have been convicted of a crime. Women who were high TV-violence viewers in childhood were more likely to have thrown something at their partners, to have responded to someone who made them angry with aggression, and to have committed some kind of criminal act. These women were four times more likely to have been violent against another adult (Huesmann *et al.* 2003).

The mechanism by which these TV watching children would become at higher risk to be aggressive has three components. Firstly, they are more likely to acquire notions about a hostile world. They are more likely to think that the world is full of 'baddies' who need 'sorting out'. This should remind you of the hostile attribution bias we discussed earlier. Secondly, continuing exposure to violence on TV is likely to lead to the acquisition of scripts for social problem solving that focus on violence. Children might become more inclined to believe that violence is an effective way of sorting out a difficult situation. Thirdly, children who watch a lot of violence on TV could acquire the normative belief that violence is normal and not only an effective but also an appropriate response to certain situations.

Violent video games

Exposure to violence carries the element of self-selection: those who like violent films might also look for violent content on the Internet, and play violent video games. There are theories that suggest that intense exposure to violent video games would be an enabler for real life aggression. The social modelling theory would certainly apply whereas excitation transfer might also explain the occurrence of certain aggressive behaviours soon after exposure to a violent video game. Extensive play of such games might 'normalise' aggression and therefore alter the way in which social information is processed. On the other hand,

---

Effects of TV violence in real-life aggression

Short-term effect
Individuals acting out what they have seen on television. This can be explained by *excitation transfer* (watching violence on television increases arousal and that might facilitate further, but possibly unrelated aggression); *priming* (watching violence makes people think, and fantasise about violence and that makes violence more likely to occur); or *imitation* (people seek to do in real life what they see on television).

Long-term effect
Children (rather than adolescents or adults) are particularly
sensitive to this. In particular children who watch a lot of
television, who prefer violent programmes, and who think that
the depiction of violence is realistic and 'true to life' are more
likely to be aggressive as adults. Berkowitz (1993) ascribes this
to observational learning of cognitions (such as scripts, beliefs,
and biases) that facilitate aggression.

there is the Freudian concept of 'catharsis'. That, simply put,
is letting off steam, so that rather than inducing aggression,
playing such games might actually be a way of getting rid of
negative affect in a relatively harmless manner (Bensley and Van
Eenwyk 2001).

Bensley and Van Eenwyk conducted an analysis of 28 research
studies. They found that among young children (4–8 years old)
aggressive video game play was often followed by a brief episode
of aggressive play straight afterwards. This is reminiscent of
the short-term effect that is regularly found for exposure to TV
violence and can be explained by imitation or excitation transfer.
However, this effect was not found for other age groups. Overall
Bensley and Van Eenwyk could not demonstrate a strong link
between violent video games and subsequent violence in real
life. The inconclusive nature of the research findings led Bensley
and Van Eenwyk (2001) to argue that 'current research evidence
is not supportive of a major concern that violent video games
lead to real-life violence'. However, they also warn that as video
games become more realistic and sophisticated this situation
might well change in the future.

Aggression in groups: deindividuation

Lost in a crowd individuals behave differently. Being part of a
large group is conducive to *deinvididuation*. Deindividuation is
a state of lowered self-awareness. It tends to occur when there
also is heightened arousal and it may bring about a temporal
reduction of our sense of personal identity. That might work as
a de-inhibitor for aggression.

Deinvidiuation is related to two other aspects that increase the
risk of violence. The first is *depersonalisation*. That refers to a state
in which the world seems less real, as if in a dream-like state.
Individuals who are engaged in high level sports or other high
arousal activities sometimes report a trance-like state. When that
kind of state brings out top performances psychologists tend to
speak of *flow*. Depersonalisation is as it were the negative side of
flow, when any sense of personal responsibility is diminished and

individuals fail to appreciate that despite their subjective state, they remain accountable for their actions.

Dehumanisation is an aspect that impinges on deindividuation, and refers to the process by which others (such as other ethnic groups, or supporters of rival sports teams) are being degraded. In most societies there are groups on the fringe of society that are to some extent dehumanised. These often are the homeless, the mentally disordered, those with disabilities or illegal immigrants. They are regarded almost as 'lesser' human beings. Being the subject of dehumanisation makes these groups significantly more likely to be on the receiving end of crime.

In the nineteenth century Gustav Le Bon (1895) discussed deindividuation as a process in which a collective consciousness takes possession over the individual. Individuals are then thrown back to a more primitive state and are, as it were, reduced to puppets acting out the violent mind of the crowd as a whole.

Deindividuation is more likely to occur when certain criteria are met. Firstly, a feeling of anonymity is conducive to deindividuation and rule-breaking behaviour. Immersion in a large group of people increases anonymity, whereas the Internet offers varying degrees of anonymity as well. Anonymity can also be achieved via the wearing of hoods, masks or non-transparent sunglasses. Arousal is another factor that can enhance a state of less self-awareness, which can also be exacerbated by alcohol or drugs (Zimbardo 1969). Rather than individuals losing their mind, Zimbardo argues that the loss of individuality removed internalised moral restraints. They continue to behave rationally.

Riot police. Deindividuation could occur in police operations.
Photo courtesy of Jan Brayley (Hampshire Constabulary).

Diener *et al.* (1976) carried out the so-called 'trick or treat' study. They observed 1,300 children in a naturalistic setting, namely when they, on Hallowe'en engaged in 'trick or treat'. This involves children dressed up in Hallowe'en outfits knocking on doors, for which they expect to be rewarded often in the form of sweets. Diener and colleagues found that children who wore outfits that made them unrecognisable (for instance because of masks) displayed more anti-normative behaviour, such as stealing. At first sight that is a classic case of deindividuation affecting rule-breaking behaviour (see Key study).

However, in their comprehensive review of studies on deindividuation, Postmes and Spears (1998) argue that the *trick or treat* study was unable to establish whether children were more likely to steal due to the fact that there was less self-awareness as a state, or that these children were mindful of the fact that when disguised, they might simply be less likely to be recognised, and hence, to get caught. The latter explanation would suggest that these children were in fact rather rational actors, rather than individuals lost in the ambiance of a special context.

Conclusion

When assessing the causes of crime we initially looked at biological and genetic theories. Subsequently learning theory was examined and it was demonstrated that social or vicarious learning can be powerful shapers for behaviour. Moral reasoning and social information processing featured subsequently, and

Key study: Hallowe'en and deindividuation

Effects of deindividuation variables on stealing among Hallowe'en trick or treaters

Aim
To explore how deindividuation affects children's likelihood of stealing.

Method
Participants
1,352 children from Seattle, US who were trick or treating on the evening of Hallowe'en. The children visited one of the 27 homes throughout the city selected for the study.

Procedure
In the entrance area of each home was a low table with two bowls. The candy bowl contained bite-sized individually wrapped candy bars. The money bowl contained small change. An unobtrusive observer observed the children's behaviour through a peephole.

An experimenter greeted the children and told each child 'You (or each of you) may take *one* of the candies. I have to go back to my work in another room'. The observer recorded how many sweets each child actually took and whether any money was taken and whether children were alone or in a group.

There are three experimental conditions but for brevity we will discuss only two:

* In the *anonymous condition* the children did not have to identify themselves and as Hallowe'en outfits tend to involve masks and face paint, this is a naturally occurring state of anonymity. In the *non-anonymous condition*, the experimenter asked each child for their name and where they lived.
* Children came to the house either in *groups* or *alone*. This a naturalistic variable, not controlled by the experimenters. It makes the experiment in part quasi-experimental.

Results
The 1,352 children committed 416 transgressions (of those, 65.4 per cent took extra sweets, 13.9 per cent took money, and 20.7 per cent took both). Both deindividuation variables led to increases in antisocial behaviour. Least likely to transgress were those who were not anonymous and by themselves (7.8 per cent). In contrast, 20 per cent of those who had given their name and address, but were in a group, did transgress. Children who were on their own and anonymous transgressed in 21.4 per cent of cases. The naughtiest were anonymous children in a group: 57.2 per cent took extra sweets, money or both.

Percentage of children's transgressions

Condition	% Transgressing
Non-anonymous	
• Alone	7.5
• Group	20.8
Anonymous	
• Alone	21.4
• Group	57.2

Discussion

Anonymity and belonging to a group have a powerful effect on the behaviour of group members. The behaviour of the first child to act is also important as he or she becomes a 'model' for the behaviour of subsequent children in the group. When the first child transgresses, in over 75 per cent of cases, at least one other child in the group does the same. If the first child does not break the rules, there is a 90 per cent chance that the other children will not do so either.

On an ethical note, remember that participants:

• did not know they were part of the study;
• could not give informed consent;
• could not withdraw at any point;
• were not debriefed.

Source: Diener et al. (1976).

it was found that the hostile attribution bias can explain how certain encounters become characterised by aggression. We then looked at the psychology of aggression and found a good number of theories that link aggression to cognition, and arousal, but also to heat, and to television, as well as deindividuation and dehumanisation, a notion to which we return when we discuss prison psychology. There is no doubt that aggression is a multi-faceted phenomenon: it is hardly ever the case that aggression and violence can simply be ascribed to one single factor. Instead, most of the time it is likely that factors operate in conjunction, with temperamental and cognitive factors combining with situational factors to bring about aggressive behaviour.

In a way, predicting violence is like predicting lightning. We know that lightning comes with thunder and meteorologists can predict with reasonable accuracy where thunderstorms might occur. Psychologists can do the same regarding aggression. But just as weather forecasters are unable to pinpoint exactly which house or tree will be hit by a thunderbolt, psychologists are unable to predict exactly who will become aggressive and when. Individual predictions of aggression are extremely difficult. It is well known however, that previous violence is one of the best predictors for future violence. The saying is that lightning does not strike twice; repeated victimisation of violence (in particular domestic violence) is sadly all too common.

Chapter 3

Solving crime

The nature of police work

What do the police do? The police mainly perform two functions. The first is the maintenance of public order. The police walk the streets and deal with any problems that they encounter. Those problems can be crimes, but also individuals who need help, disputes between neighbours and traffic situations. This is often called community policing, or neighbourhood policing, and it is characterised by police officers visibly patrolling local neighbourhoods. The other police function is to investigate crime. Bayley (1994) estimated that about two thirds of all officers are engaged in patrol duties, i.e. they are bobbies on the beat. Their job is reactive: they respond to calls and needs from the public. Most of the time, these calls are not, or not directly, related to crime. Perhaps one in four reports actually concerns a crime.

Most of the incidents the police deal with are hardly exciting. Many are so-called cat-in-a-tree situations, varying requests from the public: an old woman suffering from Alzheimer's disease might call the police frequently about imagined crimes. A person might phone the police because they think their neighbour has fallen out of bed and might be hurt. A parent might ring the police because their teenage daughter did not come home at the time that she said she would be. And so on and so on. Much police time is therefore spent on reassuring citizens and the use of persuasion rather than force to solve problems.

At the same time, we must appreciate the uncertainty and risk involved in a normal day's work. The tawdry routine of the day may at any point be interrupted. There might be a shooting, a traffic incident involving deaths, or a toddler, fallen from a balcony sustaining horrific injuries. Bayley gives an example:

Two officers responded urgently to the report of a man with a gun fighting with others at a housing project. The officers found a large middle-aged Native American man standing numbly on the sidewalk, his son on the ground, bleeding from a shoulder wound and a torn ear. The other man with a cut and bruised face stood nearby not far from a discarded .22-caliber rifle. They had no idea who the culprits were or whether they were still nearby. (Bayley 1994: 25)

Reassurance policing

The mainstay of police activity is reassurance policing. Reassurance policing must be visible. Police officers must be visibly active and available within local communities and must be seen to be tackling crime and disorder, they must also be seen to listen to the concerns of the citizens. In addition, reassurance policing is about accessibility. That means that the police should be easy to find, and their services should be of a low threshold. Finally, reassurance policing should be characterised by familiarity: local people should know their local police officers and vice versa (Herrington and Millie 2006). It should move the police away from only talking to citizens when there is trouble.

Traffic police. Much policing is not to do with crime, but with traffic. *Photo courtesy of Jan Brayley (Hampshire Constabulary).*

Reassurance policing in theory sounds exactly what we would like the police to do. However, when reassurance policing was introduced in a number of areas in England, an evaluation showed an interested mixed bag of findings. In seven of the ten areas surveyed, people on average indicated that there was less crime than a year before. Fear of crime was reduced as well. However, figures of recorded crime did not actually decrease, but despite that people said that the quality of policing had improved (Morris 2006).

These are interesting findings: there were, seemingly, no fewer crimes, but public confidence had improved regardless. Bayley argues that this is not an exception:

> The police do not prevent crime. This is one of the best kept secrets of modern life. Experts know it, the police know it, but the public does not know it. Yet the police pretend that they are society's best defence against crime and continually argue that if they are given more resources, especially personnel, they will be able to protect communities against crime. This is a myth. (Bayley 1994: 3)

Take the cops off the streets and what happens? Nothing!

The lack of a relation between police patrol and crime levels was most compellingly demonstrated by an experiment in Kansas City in the US. Kelling *et al.* (1974) sought to challenge the view that the presence of police officers on patrol should inhibit criminal activity. In the city of Kansas 15 local beat areas (comprising 32 square miles with almost 150,000 citizens) became part of a unique experiment. For one year, these areas were subjected to either reactive, proactive or control beat patrolling. In the control beats, policing continued as usual. In reactive beats, the police were taken off the streets. They would only enter the area by car in response to calls for services. Thus, in the reactive condition, police visibility was reduced to a minimum, but police availability was retained. Police response times to emergencies remained at the same level. In the third category, the proactive beats, police patrolling was carried out with at least double intensity.

The researchers measured a range of outcome data. These included surveys of citizens regarding victimisation, their attitude towards the police, and their perceptions of crime. The views of local businesses were also sought. Reported crime and traffic data, data on arrests and other police activity were utilised as well. Finally response times were measured and a great number of interviews were undertaken with police officers involved.

Beforehand it was agreed that if crime were to rise in the 'low-police' reactive beats, then the experiment would be terminated. In fact, the experiment carried on for the whole year. The results were sobering. Crime, either measured by victimisation surveys or by reported crime data, did not vary by type of patrol. In addition, citizens' perception of the police or their fear of crime was unaffected as well. These findings challenge our understanding of policing. Police officers themselves attach great value to the patrol activity, and often find it a core function. But its benefits are difficult to measure. Is having bobbies on the beat only to do with reassurance?

Criminal investigation

Criminal investigation by the police is usually carried out by plain-clothed detectives. They are less tied to an area or a daily schedule than beat officers. Within criminal investigation a substantial degree of specialisation has taken place. Scenes of crime officers (SOCOs) are trained in securing evidence from crime scenes. That can be anything ranging from fingerprints, traces of hair, foreign objects or footprints. Similarly, specialist units tend to investigate transnational crime, such as drugs trafficking. Complex organised crime is dealt with by specialist organisations such as SOCA, the Serious Organised Crime Agency (see. http://www.soca.gov.uk), or the Serious Fraud Office (SFO, see http://www.sfo.gov.uk).

DNA profiling

DNA evidence has been called the 'greatest breakthrough in forensic science since fingerprinting' (Townley and Ede 2004: 8). DNA stands for Deoxyribonucleic acid. It is a complex molecule in the shape of a helix and found in virtually every cell in the body. It contains the genetic information that we receive from our parents and pass on to our children. Any person's DNA is unique with the exception of identical twins.

On crime scenes, DNA is often obtained from blood, semen or other physical traces, such as saliva. Finding DNA at a crime scene is a valuable piece of evidence. However, you must understand that DNA is not used to determine physical or psychological characteristics of the offender. The DNA characteristic used is its uniqueness. The key to the success of DNA profiling is whether a so-called match can be found.

A DNA sample obtained from a crime scene (or a suspect) can be compared to DNA stored in a database. In the UK, the National DNA Database stores such samples. Over 3 million

DNA profiles from individuals are on the National DNA Database (NDNAD) and this number continues to increase (Parliamentary Office of Science and Technology 2006). More than 5 per cent of the population is represented in the database, mostly from people who have been involved in the criminal justice system but also from volunteers. In addition, the database holds over 200,000 samples obtained at crime scenes that are as yet unsolved. These samples lie in waiting, ready for a match from a new sample.

Criminal investigation benefits greatly from this database. Whenever DNA is collected at a crime scene, there is about a 45 per cent probability that it will match with a profile in the database. That confirms the identity of the person from whom the sample came. In addition, a serious crime where DNA has been obtained is twice as likely to be solved as one where no DNA was obtained. However, we must realise that most crimes are investigated without obtaining DNA. In fact, only 1 per cent of all recorded crimes involved a DNA sample. After all, many crimes are such that no DNA could possibly be obtained.

Importantly, DNA evidence is not only valuable in securing convictions. It can also be used to exonerate people who were convicted for a crime they did not commit. Thus, DNA evidence can overturn miscarriages of justice, most famously the so-called Cardiff Three (see Chapter 4).

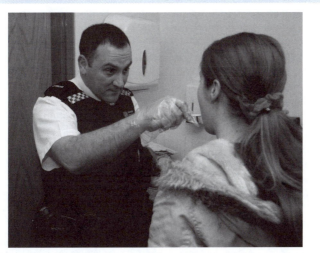

DNA swipe. DNA profiling has transformed criminal investigation. An officer takes a sample from an individual.
Photo courtesy of Jan Brayley (Hampshire Constabulary).

Psychology and investigative interviewing

The nature and purpose of police interviewing has seen a sea of change over the last 25 years. Police interviewing of suspects used to be characterised by *interrogation*, with its primary aim to obtain a confession. Interrogation implies a confrontational process, as well as a potentially flawed mindset: the police already 'know' that their suspect is the guilty person; they just have to 'prove' it. Interrogation is a hostile technique and not without risk. Gudjonsson (2007) explains that it tends to involve an over-reliance on behavioural signs of deception and the use of trickery and deceit. These factors make so-called false confessions more likely to occur. As we shall see later, false confessions can occur for a variety of reasons, and the police are not always to blame.

Psychologist in profile

'My work has always involved teaching police officers'

Dr Becky Milne
Chartered Forensic Psychologist
University of Portsmouth

'I studied psychology in Portsmouth and did my PhD there as well. To be honest, psychology was not my first choice. I actually wanted to study ophthalmic optics to become an eye doctor but I didn't get the required A-level results! That is how I ended up studying psychology instead. My third year dissertation was on facial disfigurement. I looked at children's stereotypes. Children at various ages respond differently to other children with imperfections, and such things greatly interest me.

My PhD was on the police interviewing of children and vulnerable witnesses using the cognitive interview. That is an interview technique that yields better quality information from victims and witnesses than a standard police interview. I then got a job at the Institute for Criminal Justice Studies at the University of Portsmouth.

My work has always involved teaching police officers. I train police officers in the techniques of interviewing of witnesses and victims. In addition I am involved nationally in developing guidelines on how police officers and social workers should interview children and vulnerable witness. My research on the effectiveness of the cognitive interview plays a role in that and it is good to see it applied in practice.

An interesting aspect of my work involves giving interviewing advice to the police. I recently advised a police team who were about to interview a mother whose baby child had died. We spoke at length about how the interview should be carried out in order to be sensitive to her grief but still effective. The involvement of a psychologist in such cases is vital. Psychologists can make a difference in such cases and it is very fulfilling to be a part of that.'

The *Police and Criminal Evidence Act 1984* was an important step in improving police interviewing. Since the Act became law, interviews with suspects are tape-recorded. That opens these interviews up to scrutiny, and that alone reduces the chance of inappropriate or unethical interviewing to occur. Prior to 1984 it was difficult to know exactly how interviewing occurred, although Irving (1980) carried out a significant observational study. He witnessed 60 police interviews and found them to be characterised by manipulation. The tactics he observed included:

- Pointing out that denying is futile;
- Pretending that the police had more evidence against the suspect than was the case;
- Minimising the seriousness of the offence, so as to facilitate a confession;
- Working on the offender's self-esteem;
- Convincing suspects that confessing to the crime was in their best interests.

Source: Milne and Bull (1999)

The first to investigative police interviews that had been taped was Baldwin in 1993. He examined no less than 600 taped interviews and found police interviews less manipulative than before. However, he also found them rather unfocused:

Most were short and surprisingly amiable discussions in which it often seemed that officers were rather tentative in putting allegations to a suspect ... Even if a suspect denied the allegation, no challenge was made by the interviewers in almost 40 per cent of cases. (Baldwin 1993: 331)

Baldwin (1993) therefore called the traditional police interview 'thoroughly deficient' as an objective search for the truth. It was time for a new approach.

The cognitive interview and the enhanced cognitive interview

The technique known as the cognitive interview was developed in order to optimise information in interview situations. It is informed by the psychology of memory. Memory is reconstructive. It is fallible and can be affected by suggestive questioning and by post-event information, as demonstrated in a highly compellingly study by Loftus and Palmer (1974, see Key study).

Key study: Can words change memories?

Reconstruction of automobile destruction: an example of the interaction between language and memory

Aim
To examine the effect of leading questions on participants' memory of a road traffic accident.

Experiment 1
Method
Forty-five students were shown a 30 second videotape depicting a road traffic accident. After watching the film, the participants were given a questionnaire. The critical question asked the participants about the speed at which they thought the car was travelling. Nine participants were asked, 'How fast were the cars going when they *hit* each other?' The remaining participants were asked the same critical question with the word 'hit' replaced with either 'smashed', 'collided', 'bumped', or 'contacted'.

Results
Speed estimates for the verbs used

Verb	Mean speed estimates
Smashed	40.8
Collided	39.3
Bumped	38.1
Hit	34.0
Contacted	31.8

The results show that the verb used in the leading question significantly influenced participants' estimate of the speed of the car.

Discussion
The authors give two explanations for this finding. Firstly, there may be a response-bias, meaning that the verb *biases* a response towards a higher estimate. Secondly, the leading question causes a specific change in the participant's memory of the event.

Experiment 2
One week later, the participants returned and, without seeing the film again, were asked a series of questions about the accident. The critical question was 'Did you see any broken glass?' The students had to respond either 'yes' or 'no'. Crucially, there was no broken glass in the accident.

Results

Responses to the question 'did you see any broken glass?'

	Verb		
	Smashed	Hit	Control
Yes	16	7	6
No	34	43	44

Participants in the 'smashed' condition gave significantly higher 'yes' responses than participants in the 'hit' or control conditions: they reported having seen broken glass where in fact, there was none.

Discussion

As a consequence of these results Loftus and Palmer propose that two kinds of information influence a person's memory of an event. First, there is the person's memory of the event; and, second the information supplied *after* the event. Over time, this information combines to make one memory.

Source: Loftus and Palmer (1974).

Memory relies on encoding (how an event is perceived and how the information is processed), storage (the extent and way it is kept in long term memory), and retrieval (how the information is accessed when required). At the stage of a police interview, it is too late to affect encoding which obviously happened when the 'to be remembered' event took place. Storage cannot be directly affected either, although obviously, the sooner an interview can be held, the more likely it is that storage will remain relatively unaffected. Retrieval, however, can be facilitated and the cognitive interview seeks to do that.

In its original form the cognitive interview comprised four instructions (Fisher and Geiselman 1992). The first instruction is *report everything*. It encourages interviewees to report everything they remember. Even if they think it is not important or trivial the interviewee is encouraged to mention it anyway. The report everything instruction should lead to more correct information being reported (Milne and Bull 1999).

The second instruction involves *the mental reinstatement of context*. It asks interviewees to reconstruct in their minds the context (both physical and personal) of the witnessed event. Milne and Bull (1999) explain what such an instruction can be like:

Put yourself back to the same place where you saw the armed robbery. Create a picture in your mind of the bank. Think of where you were in the bank. How were you feeling at the time? What did you hear? What did you smell? Think of all the people who were present. Think about all the objects in the bank. Get a really good picture in your mind and then tell me everything you can remember without leaving anything out. All that pops into your head, tell me. (Milne and Bull 1999: 35)

As memory can be state dependent the mental reinstatement of the context should facilitate recall.

The third instruction is *change perspectives*. It invites interviewees to report events from a different perspective, such as another witness or from different angle. Anderson and Pichert (1978) found that when participants had to recall details of a story involving a burglary, they remembered more when they were asked to change perspectives. When they told their story again, but this time from the house buyer's perspective, further information was recalled. That prompted Fisher and Geiselman to include this in the cognitive interview.

Finally, the interviewee is encouraged to recall in more than one temporal order. When people narrate a story, they stick by and large to the order of events. When information is actually in a different order, such as for instance in reverse order, starting at the end and working towards the beginning of the event, people might recall more information. Geiselman and Callot (1990) indeed found that witnesses who were asked to recall an event twice in chronological order performed less well than those who were asked to recall in chronological order once and once in reverse order.

The enhanced cognitive interview (ECI) consists of the four techniques discussed above but these are wrapped around a number of further components. Fisher *et al.* (1989) found that although the four techniques should facilitate recall, they will

Remembering

The process of remembering involves the processes of encoding, storage and retrieval. Although they tend to serve us quite well in our daily life, these processes are subject to error and distortion. Encoding is limited by attention, and storage requires processing in working memory with its limited capacity. Finally, retrieval is subject to failure as well. Evidence of that is the so-called 'tip of the tongue' phenomenon.

Police interviewing. The interviewing of victims and witness is a key police skill.
Photo courtesy of Jan Brayley (Hampshire Constabulary).

also work effectively if performed within a competent interview structure. The ECI therefore represents more of a complete package. It consists of seven phases.

A number of experiments have demonstrated the effects of the cognitive and the enhanced cognitive interview. Generally, they

The phases of the enhanced cognitive interview

Phase 1 – Greet and establish rapport.

Phase 2 – Explain the aims of the interview.

Phase 3 – Initiate a free recall
- context reinstatement;
- open-ended questions;
- pauses;
- report everything;
- appropriate non-verbal behaviour.

Phase 4 – Questioning
- no guessing;
- 'it's ok to say "I don't know" ';
- 'it's ok to say "I don't understand" ';
- open and closed questions.

Phase 5 – Varied and extensive recall
- change the temporal order;
- change perspectives;
- focus on all senses (visual, hearing, smell, taste and touch).

Phase 6 – Summary.

Phase 7 – Closure.

Adapted from Milne and Bull (1999).

find that the extent of correct information reported, increases. In addition, it is usually found that the number of incorrect details or confabulations does not tend to increase. The latter is of crucial importance. If the cognitive interview would yield increased correct as well as incorrect information, its advantage could easily be overshadowed by its negative side effects.

Geiselman *et al.* (1986) showed 51 adults (ranging from 20 to 52 years of age) one of two films of about four minutes. Both were police training videos and showed a form of violent crime. Nine experienced detectives interviewed these 51 participants. One group used the cognitive interview, and the other experimental group was interviewed via their 'regular' interview procedure. The interviewees subjected to the cognitive interview produced over five pieces more correct information. That was a 15 per cent differential between the 'regular' group and the cognitive interview group. The extent of incorrect information was the same between both groups.

Fisher *et al.* (1989) were the first to test the success of the enhanced cognitive interview in practice. They analysed audio recordings of real life witness interviews and found the interviewers who had been trained in using the ECI obtained 47 per cent more information than before they had been trained.

Interviewing vulnerable witnesses

It has been argued that cognitive interviewing might not be suitable for all types of witness or victims. You might wonder whether traumatised victims, the very young and those with learning difficulties would be able to carry out the instructions contained in the cognitive interview. Fritzon (2005) quotes Tully and Cahill who refer to a number of weaknesses that can increase the risk of incorrect testimony by people with a learning disability.

- *Acquiescing to leading questions.* It might be assumed that the interviewer actually knows all the answers and leading questions can be taken to contain the 'right' answer.
- *Confabulation.* Even small amounts of pressure might prompt a vulnerable interviewee to fill in parts of an account they are not sure about.
- *Upgrading of responses.* Inarticulate or ambiguous statements can be unwittingly 'clarified' incorrectly by the interviewer.

- *Forced choice alternatives.* Two options are offered (e.g. 'Was the car blue or white?'), and the interviewee incorrectly chooses one in the absence of the correct answer (if the car was in fact green).
- *Cycles of 'don't know'.* Not knowing the answer to a series of questions can be embarrassing. When suddenly there is an answer following a number of unanswered questions, it is important not to accept it uncritically.
- *Tendency to say 'yes', rather than 'no'.* People with learning disabilities, when faced with a forced choice question are more inclined to say 'yes' and agree with the interviewer.

Making sure that vulnerable witnesses can provide valid testimony is a key objective of the criminal justice system.

Key study: Interviewing people with learning disabilities

Using the cognitive interview with adults with mild learning disabilities

Aim
To examine the effectiveness of cognitive interviewing on adults with mild learning disabilities; and to compare their recall of an event with the general population.

Method
Participants
Thirty-four men and 13 women with mild learning disabilities (mean age 35 years) based at six day centres in either London or Portsmouth. Thirteen men and 25 women (mean 39 years) recruited from the general population via newspaper advertisement and local job centres.

Procedure
Participants were shown a three-minute video of an accident in which a boy was knocked down by a car on his way to school. The video was shown to up to eight participants at one time who were told 'watch carefully as you will be asked what you think about it later'. Participants were randomly assigned to either the cognitive interview or standard interview condition and were interviewed approximately 24 hours later.

Results
All participants interviewed using a cognitive interview recalled more accurate details than those in the standard interview condition. However, more confabulations by the learning disabled group were made in the cognitive interview condition compared to those who were learning disabled in the standard interview condition.

SOLVING CRIME

Discussion

Whilst the general population group were significantly more reliable overall, the authors point out that the accuracy ratios of the learning disabilities group did not drop below 74 per cent. Further, the cognitive interview enhanced the recall of adults with mild learning disabilities who outperformed participants in the general population in the standard interview condition. Therefore, the study does not support the notion that people with learning disabilities are unreliable witnesses and the cognitive interview can be a useful means of helping learning disabled individuals to provide reliable information.

Source: Milne *et al.* (1999).

A study by Milne *et al.* (1999) is therefore of relevance. They successfully applied the cognitive interview with adults with mild learning disabilities (see Key study). That is an important step forward in achieving justice for vulnerable people who come into contact with the criminal justice system as a victim or witness.

Detection of deception

Within criminal justice the detection of deception has obvious relevance. It not only will help identify the offender who maintains their innocence in the police station or in court, but it might also help in identifying false confessions and will be useful to identify false allegations as well. Deception is defined as 'a successful or unsuccessful deliberate attempt, without forewarning, to create in another a belief which the communicator considers to be untrue' (Vrij 2000: 6).

There are three ways to catch a liar. The first is to look at their non-verbal behaviour. The second is to analyse the content of what they say, and the third is to look at physiological variables, such as blood pressure, heart rate, sweating, etcetera (Memon *et al.* 2003).

Non-verbal clues to deception

The short answer is that there is no general cue to spot a lie. Thus, staring at the ceiling, covering the mouth or speaking in a high pitched voice are not fail proof indicators that someone is lying. Thus, there is no 'Pinocchio's nose'.* DePaulo and Morris

*Pinocchio was the fairy tale little boy whose nose grew every time he told a lie.

explain why assuming that there would be any tell-tale sign would be too simplistic: 'The real world of behavioural cues is not like this. Lying is not a distinct psychopathological process with its own unique behavioural indicators. It does matter how liars feel and how they think.' (DePaulo and Morris 2004).

Vrij argues that there are three lying-related aspects that might help in catching liars. These are emotions, so-called content complexity and attempted behavioural control. Firstly, telling a lie might invoke strong emotions, such as guilt or fear of being found out. Fear might manifest itself via speech errors or a higher pitched voice. But many liars will not be afraid when they lie so that these behavioural cues will not always appear.

Secondly lying and sustaining that lie might be complicated. Sustaining a complicated lie is a cognitively complex task. When engaged in such tasks, most people show increased gaze aversion (looking away) and fewer limb movements. People will pause for longer, simply because they need to think before giving an answer. Thus, complexity is key as complexity affects behaviour.

Finally, liars are likely to engage in impression management. If you do not want to be unmasked as a liar, it is likely that you will try to avoid giving away any signs that you are in fact lying. That means that liars tend to try to correspond to their idea of how an honest person would present themselves in their situation. But that might make their behaviour look contrived, detached and not entirely convincing. Because of the interplay of these factors, there is no standard set of clues to identify a liar.

The good news is, however, that both Vrij (2000) and DePaulo et al. (2003) found that certain behaviours are more likely to occur when lying. These are a high pitch voice and an increased rate of speech errors, whereas so called illustrators (arm and hand movements to modify or supplement what is being said) and hand and finger movements occur less often.

Interestingly, the face does not offer any consistent clues into lying, nor do signs of nervousness. Gaze aversion and fidgeting do not occur more often when a person is lying. The law enforcement officer who relies on those is therefore likely to get it wrong. Altogether it is advisable to not over-rely on non-verbal cues to uncover lying.

The over-reliance on non-verbal clues might help explain why law enforcement officers are generally found to be poor at the detection of deception. That is surprising. You might expect people who deal with deceptive behaviour for a living to be 'tuned' to lies, and to be able to spot them better than most people. The reality is different. Police officers hardly perform better than chance when deciding whether someone is lying. It is likely due to the fact that signs of nervousness are taken to be signs of dishonesty (Memon *et al.* 2003).

Content analysis

Telling a lie is typically verbal behaviour. It seems therefore to make sense to look at that verbal message to find clues for deception. A technique called *statement validity analysis* has been devised to do just that. A constituent of this technique is Criteria Based Content Analysis (CBCA). It assumes that when people relate an event that actually happened to them or that they witnessed, they will tell it in a different way from an event that they made up or have been coached or coerced to tell. It is often assumed that fabricated stories are less colourful, less vivid and contain fewer details than truthful accounts. CBCA is a systematic attempt to assess that. It analyses statements on a large number of criteria. These include its logical structure, and various specifics of the account, such as the inclusion of details. Apart from the specific content of the event, motivational criteria are also examined. These include spontaneous corrections (such as 'he was wearing black shoes. No! Hang on, no, I think they were actually blue') and raising doubts about one's own testimony (such as 'I'm just not sure that I recall it all correctly but I seem to remember that he was wearing blue socks. I think.'). CBCA is often used in assessing the account of children who may have been sexually abused. In such accounts, a forgiving attitude towards the perpetrator is taken as a sign of truthfulness. A 'coached' incriminating statement would be less likely to contain a pardoning attitude to the perpetrator.

The method, as long as it is carried out by trained specialists with a good deal of knowledge of the specifics of the case to which it is applied, seems to work reasonably well. Vrij (2005) looked at 37 studies on CBCA and found average accuracy rates of 73 per cent for true accounts and 72 per cent for false accounts. That is substantially better than just chance, but obviously far from fail proof (Köhnken 2004).

Physiological ways of catching liars: the polygraph

The polygraph is a scientific measuring device that displays fluctuations of various types of bodily activity. These often include sweating of the fingertips and blood pressure. Technically, the term 'lie detector' for a polygraph is not accurate: the device cannot detect lies. It can however, detect telling physiological changes when certain answers are given. The test mostly used is the so-called Comparison Question Test (CQT). In a questioning session so-called 'relevant questions' and 'control questions' are put to the suspect. Relevant questions concern the crime under investigation. Control questions are general questions to which most respondents (regardless of whether they are guilty or not) are expected to be inclined to lie. They are generic in nature, generally vague and cover long periods of time, but do not pertain to the crime in question. They are questions such as 'Have you ever tried to hurt someone to get revenge?' These questions are intended to increase arousal, and that will show on the polygraph, via sweating or blood pressure measurements. The assumption is that guilty suspects will lie (and get nervous) answering both the generic control questions and the specific relevant questions. Innocent suspects will (literally) sweat over the control questions, but can honestly and calmly deny the relevant questions. Therefore, innocent suspects should show a different physiological profile when answering those questions (Granhag and Vrij 2005).

The empirical research into the polygraph's ability to differentiate between truth tellers and liars has not yielded highly positive results. This is partly due to methodological difficulties. There are laboratory studies in simulated settings but they are unlikely to capture the essence of what the polygraph seeks to measure: when research does not involve real suspects, we cannot expect anyone to become very nervous when they answer certain questions.

The best way, therefore, to test the polygraph is in the real world. But here we have the problem of 'ground truth'. Suspects are often subjected to the polygraph because we do not know for certain whether they are guilty or not. That makes independent verification very difficult. Tests in the real world are often small scale, with very few participants. That also makes generalisation hazardous. What they tend to find, however, it that lying is detected better than telling the truth. When the suspect is lying,

Table 3.1 Assumptions regarding suspects' arousal during the Comparison Question Test (see text for further explanation)

	Relevant questions (specific)	Control questions (general)
Guilty suspect	Increased	Increased
Innocent suspect	Not increased	Increased

Source: Granhag and Vrij (2005).

that is detected over 80 per cent of the time. However, that does mean that one in five guilty persons manages to 'beat the test'. More disturbing is the finding that the test only tends to correctly identify the truthful person about 60 per cent of the time. Thus, two out of five actually truthful people would still fail the polygraph test. Those margins of error are very substantial (Granhag and Vrij 2005). In summary we cannot recommend the polygraph as a reliable device for the detection of deception. It simply gets it wrong too often. At present the polygraph is not legally admissible evidence in the UK. Given the evidence on its effectiveness, that is probably for the best.

False confessions

Why would anyone confess to a crime they did not commit? Kassin and Wrightsman (1985) distinguish three types of false confessions. The first type comprises *voluntary false confessions*. These are confessions that the confessor knows to be false, and not brought about by pressure. They frequently occur to protect someone else or because of a morbid desire for notoriety. Suspects also may falsely confess to a lesser crime if they think that that will avoid the detection of a more serious offence.

The second type are called *coerced compliant confessions*. Suspects frequently confess to crimes they did not commit due to torture or other forms of pressure applied by interrogators. Suspects delivering a coerced compliant confession realise that they are not telling the truth. However, the pressure can be such that they decide to say what they think the interrogators want to hear in order to be left alone. Coerced compliant confessions may occur further to false promises made by the interrogators. They might say things like 'if you won't confess we will arrest your wife', or it might be suggested that they have strong evidence against a suspect so that they might as well confess. Prior to the *Police And Criminal Evidence Act 1984*, such antics were not uncommon.

Finally, there are *coerced internalised confessions*. These are perhaps the most puzzling. Conti explains that a coerced internalised confession occurs when 'suspects who are innocent, but anxious, fatigued, pressured, or confused and then subjected to highly suggestive methods of police interrogation, actually come to believe that they committed the crime' (Conti 1999: 22). They typically occur with vulnerable suspects (for instance due to low intelligence, mental health problems, alcohol and drugs). Should they be exposed to bogus claims about evidence against them, they might come to 'remember' that they committed a crime they had, in fact, nothing to do with.

Types of false confessions

Voluntary: the suspect knows their confession is false and not caused by pressure.
Coerced compliant: a suspect yields to pressure and confesses but knows deep down they are innocent.
Coerced internalised: brought about by pressure but the suspect comes to believe that they are in fact guilty.

Source: Kassin and Wrightsman (1985).

This may seem rather far-fetched. However, an alcoholic may frequently suffer from memory lapses. The same might apply to those with certain mental illnesses. Should they be confronted with evidence that suggests that they committed a crime, they might be not unwilling to accept that, even though initially they may not have any recollections to corroborate that.

Gudjonsson (2007) argued that the construct that explains most coerced internalised false confessions is that of 'interrogative suggestibility'. Not all vulnerable suspects are equally suggestible, however naivety, low intelligence, low self-esteem, lack of assertiveness and anxiety all correlate with suggestibility. Police interview rooms can be frightening places, particularly to vulnerable suspects. It is therefore important that vulnerable suspects are protected.

In Britain therefore so-called *appropriate adult* schemes are in place. All suspects under 16 years of age and all vulnerable adults can have an appropriate adult with them during police

Volunteers

Volunteers play an increasingly important role in criminal justice. The appropriate adult, to assist vulnerable people during police interviews is one such role. Other roles involve victim support or being a 'play worker' in prison: during prison visits, many visitors bring inmates' children. Play workers ensure that for these children these visits are fun. Check out http://www. whatcanIdo.org.uk for more information on volunteer work in criminal justice.

interviews. They will often be a family member or a friend but they can also be volunteers. The appropriate adult is there as a source of support. That should reduce the chances of coerced confessions to occur. Further information on appropriate adult schemes can be found on http://www.appropriateadult.org.uk.

Offender profiling

Offender profiling is the stuff that captures the imagination. That is perhaps the case because of the juxtaposition of two extremes: unspeakably evil criminals being hunted by fiendishly clever profilers. The TV series *Profiler*, and British based *Cracker* as well as the film *Silence of the Lambs* all carry and perpetuate both extremes. Both are probably based on myth. In this section we will discuss the reality of offender profiling and the contribution it makes to criminal investigation.

Jackson and Bekerian described offender profiling as follows:

> A profile is assumed to involve the construction of a behavioural composite – a social and psychological assessment. A profile is based on the premise that the proper interpretation of crime scene evidence can indicate the personality type of the individual(s) who committed the offence. It is assumed that certain personality types exhibit similar behavioural patterns and that knowledge of these patterns can assist in the investigation of the crime and the assessment of potential suspects. (Jackson and Bekerian 1997: 3).

We discovered earlier that the analysis of a crime scene of a serious crime has become a specialist activity. It is primarily aimed at securing physical evidence and often carried out by Scenes of Crime Officers. However, offender profilers are assumed to assess a crime scene with a different perspective. They look for 'psychological' information that can provide information about the perpetrator that other forms of evidence cannot. To achieve this, it is helpful if the crime is of a certain emotive nature. Crimes that are purely acquisitive, such as burglary or bicycle theft would not be suitable as the offenders do not display any sort of individualised behaviour when committing them (Ainsworth 2001).

Two approaches to profiling are commonly identified. They are referred to as 'top down' and 'bottom up' approaches. Top down approaches work from general principles and apply those to specific cases. That works by means of heuristics, general rules about human behaviour that apply to criminal behaviour as well. In the top down approach a lot depends on the knowledge and experience of the profilers: if their skills of perception are good and they use these heuristics to good effect, a potentially useful profile can emerge. That is also why we can call this approach 'individualistic'. The advantage is that highly specialised knowledge in the head of the profiler can be effectively used. The downside is that any profile is likely to be as good as the profiler, and that their reasoning might be difficult to follow, or replicate.

The second approach can be called bottom up profiling. You can also call it data-driven, or statistical profiling. In these cases, profilers use aggregate knowledge of similar crimes and criminals to make predictions. It relies more heavily on statistical analysis and the knowledge generated is more open to scrutiny.

Offender profiles: from the 1980s to today

David Canter is perhaps Britain's foremost investigative psychologist. His first profile was that of the so-called Railway Rapist who operated in London in the 1980s, initially with an accomplice and later alone. The rapist was responsible for numerous rapes and towards the end of his series of offences killed three of his victims.

Canter worked together with detectives to produce a profile, after studying witness descriptions, case files and further to patterns they recognise in the detailed behaviour of the offender during and after the commission of the offence and their location.

His preliminary profile, produced in 1986 included the following statements:

Residence
Has lived in the area circumscribed by the first three cases since 1983.
Probably lives with wife/girlfriend, quite possibly without children.

Occupation
Probably semi-skilled or skilled job, involving weekend work or casual labour.

Character
Keeps to himself but has one or two very close male friends.
Probably very little contact with women, especially in work situation.
Has knowledge of the railway system along which attacks happened.

Criminal record
Was probably under arrest at some time between 24 October 1982 and January 1984.

When John Duffy was arrested, the match with the profile was said to be remarkable. Offender profiling was increasingly used after this early success. Years later in 2001, Duffy provided details on further offences and revealed the name of his accomplice. Duffy received another 12 years of sentence after already having been sentenced to life imprisonment. His accomplice, David Mulcahy was convicted of three murders, seven rapes and five counts of conspiracy to rape in 2001.

Since then offender profiling as performed by investigative psychologists has become highly evidence based. Consider excerpts from a profile constructed in 2004 by Alison *et al.* (2005). It involves two abductions followed by murder and one disappearance. All victims were girls between 10 and 14 years of age.

Offender's age
The offender is likely to be within an age range of 28 to 35 years (CATCHEM*). However, age has proven an extremely difficult variable to 'profile'. No suspect should be eliminated solely on the basis that he does not fall within the profiled age range. Although the average age of child sexual murderers in Boudreaux *et al.*'s (1999) study was 27 years old with the great majority under 30, the CATCHEM data indicates that when the victim's body is transported from the scene of the murder the offender's most likely age group is about 30–35 years old.

The offender's previous criminal history
The offender is likely to have a previous criminal history, including sexual offences and more general criminality such as convictions for theft and dishonesty. (...)

Canter and Kirby (1995) examined the prior convictions of 416 detected child sex offenders and report that contrary to popular belief, child molesters do not have an exclusive offence history relating to assaults on children. (...)

- 44% had previous criminal convictions;
- 86% of those had a conviction for dishonesty;
- 11% had more than eight prior convictions for offences ranging from theft and burglary to violence and indecent assault.

These excerpts demonstrate that profiling can be firmly based in evidence and highly transparent. It is clear what a profile is based on and it allows for the strength of the evidence to be assessed by those who use it.

*The CATCHEM database (Centralised Analytical Team Collating Homicide Expertise and Management) contains detailed information with respect to child homicide investigations.

Top down profiling: the work of the Federal Bureau of Investigation (FBI)

There is a strong tradition of profiling at the FBI in the US state of Virginia. Quite well known are memoirs of FBI special agents such as Ressler and Shachtman (1992) and Douglas and Ohlshaker (1997). They tend to follow a similar pattern. It goes as follows. A series of serious crimes has been committed and the killer is at large. The police run out of ideas. At a loss, they contact a relative outsider to see if they could offer some help. Enter the profiler. The profiler looks at the information and develops hypotheses regarding the actual goings on during the commission of the crime and formulates thoughts on the individual responsible for it. And in the end, these profilers are always correct and provide for a breakthrough in the investigation.

The case of the Trailside Killer that was dealt with by FBI special agent John Douglas is a good example. He described his style as follows:

> What I try to do with a case is to take in all the evidence I have the work with – the case reports, the crime-scene photos and descriptions, the victim statements or autopsy protocols – and then put myself mentally and emotionally in the head of the offender. I try to think as he does. Exactly how that happens, I'm not sure. (Douglas and Ohlshaker 1997: 151)

Several killings had occurred in a heavy wooded area with many walking paths, in a hilly area near San Francisco in the US. The offender was dubbed the Trailside Killer in the local press. FBI special agent John Douglas became involved and shared with his readers his early thoughts on the likely killer:

> I didn't think we were dealing with a good-looking charming, sophisticated type. The multiple stabbings and blitz-style attacks from the rear told me we were dealing with an asocial type (although not necessarily antisocial) who'd be withdrawn, unsure of himself, and unable to engage his victims in conversation, develop a good line, or con or coax or trick them into doing what he wanted. The hikers were all physically fit. The blitz attack was a clear indication to me that the only way he could control his intended victim was to devastate her before she could respond. (Douglas and Ohlshaker 1997: 76)

In this way, the profiler uses his assessment of the style of the attacks to predict the personal characteristics of the offender. Canter (1994) would call this an application of the continuity hypothesis. Continuity refers to the fact that the skills that offenders possess to get through life are the same skills they utilise when committing their crimes. The blitz attack in a secluded area would not be the preferred style of a charming, verbally and socially highly skilled individual. However, it is what the unskilled, unattractive individual with no confidence in engaging other people needs to resort to.

The organised offender

a) He appears to plan his murders;
b) He targets his victims;
c) He displays control at the crime scene;
d) He often uses a con or a ruse to gain control over a victim;
e) The suspect is adaptable and mobile and they learn from crime to crime;
f) He will often use restraints and rape kits;
g) He will use his own weapon and takes it away after he has finished, to avoid fingerprints;
h) He will attempt to wipe away fingerprints and blood from the crime scene; sometimes this need to avoid detection means that the suspect leaves the victim nude or decapitated;
i) He will take 'trophies' from the scene. These trophies are taken as an incorporation of the suspect's post crime fantasies and as acknowledgement of his accomplishments;
j) He will seemingly live a normal life. He may be reasonably attractive and gregarious and feel superior to almost anyone;
k) He will stage the crime to confuse the police. He will deliberately mislead the police by leaving false trails at the scene.

Source: Ressler *et al.* (1988).

This above point can be generalised into the well-known distinction of organised versus disorganised offenders. Canter explains that:

It's a simple idea once you spot it. A man who plans his life and thinks things through, who holds down a job which makes some demands on his manual or intellectual skills, will go about the business of murder rather differently from the casual, confused ne'er do well. An organised crime scene will be produced by an organized criminal. The person who leaves his victim in a hurry with no attempt at concealment is likely to have left many difficult situations in life in a hurry and known for his haphazard ways. (Canter 1994)

Thus, a key skill for profilers who utilise the bottom up approach is to assess whether a crime scene displays evidence of organised or disorganised behaviour. Has care been taken to prevent forensic evidence to be left behind? Or did the offender leave objects, and has no attempt been made to prevent or delay detection of the crime? Such clues provide information as to whether we are dealing with an organised or a disorganised offender, and that will prompt predictions in relation to intelligence, social skills, socio-economic position, and possibly their likely residence, marital and professional status, etcetera.

On the other hand, FBI data do not provide us with data on how many of the crime scenes one would qualify as organised, disorganised or mixed. We therefore cannot know whether organised and disorganised offences are ideal types or common occurrences. Because of these and other problems, Turvey simply dismisses the organised/disorganised distinction as a false dichotomy (Turvey 2002).

Evaluating FBI profiling is far from straightforward. Upon reading the memoirs by Douglas and Ressler one is left with the impression that these profilers are hardly ever wrong, and that many killers would never have been caught if it wasn't for them. But independent verification of this remains rather elusive. You can therefore wonder whether the examples selected in these books constitute a biased sample, with less successful cases left out. Pinnizotto discusses a review carried out by special agent John Douglas into the effectiveness of offender profiling as carried out by the FBI in the late 1970s. It concludes that 'All in all, investigators suggested psychological profiling had saved an estimated 594 investigative man days and all users overwhelmingly agreed that the service should be continued' (Douglas, in Copson 1995: 5). Still, this is a rather modest picture of success: framed in time saved, rather then in terms of lives saved.

Bottom up or statistical profiling

The reasoning behind statistical profiling is simple. The statistical profiler utilises knowledge from a large number of past crimes. Statistical analysis of details of those crimes can be used to arrive at predictions regarding the crime under investigation. This method is more transparent as well as more exact. Where top down profilers often litter their profiles with qualifiers such as 'probably', 'possibly', or 'not unlikely', statistical profilers are able to precisely state with what probability certain characteristics would be present in the as yet unknown offender.

The work of Anne Davies (1997) on stranger rapists is a good example. One of the research questions she addressed related to the geography of rape: how far do stranger rapists travel to commit their crimes? In order to assess this, she looked at case files from 299 cases of rape that had been committed by 71 rapists. She found that more than half of all offences were committed within three miles of the offender's home (or base, as their base is not necessarily their home). Almost a quarter of these rapists were bold enough to commit their rapes (or at least approach their victims) within half a mile from their home (see Table 3.2). Some 87% live within 10 miles. Thus, when investigating a rape committed by a stranger, it seems safe to assume that, unless there are indications otherwise, the offender is a local.

Such 'spatial' research is not without its problems. One obvious problem concerns offenders without a fixed address. They cannot really contribute to this picture. Secondly, offenders may have several anchor points or bases. One of these anchor points is likely to be their home, but another may be their work place, or the home of a friend or family member. A rapist who tends to commit his crimes after leaving work in a night shift might commit his crimes close to his workplace, but relatively far from home. Thirdly, is it probably unsafe to assume that people on holiday would never commit crimes. People can be less inhibited when on holiday abroad, and this is not unlikely to affect offending behaviour as well and it complicates the picture even further. A further complication is posed by rapists or killers who target a particular type of victim. If a rapist or killer is after street prostitutes it is inevitable that he travels to the area where street prostitutes can be found. Thus, offenders with a preference for particular victims might be travelling

Table 3.2 The distance from the offender's base to the locations where the victims were approached

Distance	Offenders (%) n=71	Offences (%) n=299
0–0.5 miles	23.9	17.4
0.5–1.0 miles	11.3	11.7
1.0–2.0 miles	21.1	22.4
2.0–3.0 miles	9.9	8.4
3.0–4.0 miles	4.2	8.7
4.0–5.0 miles	4.2	7.0
5.0–10.0 miles	12.7	12.9
Over 10 miles	12.7	11.4

Source: Davies (1997).

further, as do those who spend a great deal of effort in hunting or prowling for victims (see also Canter and Larkin 1993). Given these complications, the fact that most offenders stay close to home when they offend becomes even more impressive. In addition Davies (1997) obtained the following results when she assessed the criminal records of these stranger rapists after they had been apprehended (see Table 3.3).

Firstly, it must be emphasised that 'only' 32 per cent of stranger rapists had previous convictions for sex offences. That is an important finding: you would come across less than one in three stranger rapists, if you looked through criminal records

---

Evaluate

Are these findings valid and can they be generalised to other crimes?

Validity: most crimes are not reported, and if reported may not be solved.
Thus, the fact that most 'stranger rapists' do not have prior convictions for sex offences does not mean that they never offended before. To what extent does 'recorded convictions' measure 'previous offending'?

Generalisation: would you assume that what is true for stranger rapists is true for other sex offenders as well? Would any of these data apply to people who commit sex offences against people that they know?

Table 3.3 Recorded convictions for a number of crimes, for stranger rapists

Category of crime	Offenders with crimes in their criminal record (%)
Sexual	32
Violent	50
Robbery	23
Burglary	56
Theft	73
Criminal damage	35
Drugs	10
Other	31

Source: Davies (1997).

and only paid attention to sexual offences. Instead, they are more likely to have a criminal record that includes burglary or theft. That suggests that stranger rapists are generalists, rather than specialists who engage exclusively in sexual crimes.

Further statistical research sought to establish whether offenders who display certain behaviours at a crime scene have different characteristics from those who do not.

Davies scrutinised the victim statements of the 299 rape case files mentioned before. From that information she assessed whether the offender displayed a certain type of behaviour or not. Subsequently she established whether certain behaviours were indicative of the type of offender that displayed them. Consider Table 3.4. It shows the type of behaviours examined, and their frequency of occurring. Note that for this analysis, Davies only considered stranger rapists in which there was only a single perpetrator and the victim was always one female.

Davies tried to use this data to tell the first time rapist apart from the experienced sex offender. Some of these findings were highly significant. The best predictor for having previous convictions for rape is semen destruction: those who make sure that no semen is left, or destroy it, are most likely to have previous convictions for rape. Another interesting finding is that if a rapist does not take sighting precautions, then he is three times more likely to be a one-off offender. Rapists who took fingerprint precautions were four times as likely to have a conviction for burglary than those who did not. Sighting

Table 3.4   The frequencies of offence behaviours (n=299)

Offender's behaviour	Frequency in the offences (%)
Fingerprint precautions	15
Semen destruction	5
Sighting precautions	28
Lies to mislead	20
Departure precautions	32
Reference to the police	13
Theft from victim	40
Forced entry	25
Weapon	30
Extreme violence	20
Confidence approach	48
Alcohol	35

Source: Davies (1997).
Note Percentages exceed 100% due to multiple behaviours.

precautions tend to co-occur with fingerprint precautions, departure precautions, theft from the victim, and not using the confidence approach. Offenders who display this behaviour pattern are most likely to be experienced criminals with a past of both rape and burglary.

Keeping the peace. Much police activity involves the use of persuasion rather than force coercion.
Photo courtesy of Jan Brayley (Hampshire Constabulary).

Such findings are obviously useful in police investigation. Although they will never directly and exclusively point out the offender, they may steer police investigation, and help in prioritising suspects. Add to this the fact that most rapists live quite near the crime scene, such information might become highly relevant indeed in drawing up a 'shortlist' of potential suspects.

Activity

Classroom debate
Davies' research relies in details provided by victims. These victims are likely to be traumatised and are likely to find discussing their experience distressing. That presents an ethical concern: does the value of the research outweigh the distress caused to those who were involved in the research?

Evaluating profiling

Evaluating the success of profilers and the accuracy and utility of profiles has turned out to be a tricky business. As we saw earlier, an investigation into FBI profiling suggested positive evaluations and valuable time saved. In Britain, an important evaluation of profiling was carried out by Gudjonsson and Copson. They surveyed police investigative teams who had utilised a profiler and solicited their views on their usefulness. Copson (1995) based his analysis on 184 cases in which the advice of a profiler was sought. Most of these were murder cases (61%), followed by rape cases (22%), while cases of arson (2%), extortion (7%) and abduction (2%) also occurred.

In looking at usefulness, most police teams answered that the profile did not actually help in solving the case. A good majority of teams also said that the profiler failed to open new lines of inquiry. Most did, however, rate the profile as operationally useful. Exactly how the advice was useful is shown in Table 3.5.

Clearly, the value of the profiler's advice does not lie in directly solving crimes. If that happens, that is exceptional. Rather, a profiler may offer a new idea, or a new perspective. Even if that does not occur, a profiler's input may be valuable in reassuring that the investigative team has done all it can be expected to have done.

However, Alison et al. (2003a) warn us to be wary of even this very modest evidence of success. They argue that many profiles are phrased rather ambiguously. They often contain many statements that are not verifiable: we may never know whether they actually apply to the offender, such as when they pertain to an offender's fantasies, or their presumed subconscious urges or desires. In addition, some statements might be phrased such that they apply to a great many people and therefore are not useful in pinpointing any suspect. Such items can be such as the following: 'When faced with failure, the offender will become frustrated, and might be inclined to question his own abilities.' It sounds reasonable enough, but probably applies to many if not most people (e.g., Alison et al. 2003b). Alison and colleagues

Table 3.5 How the advice was useful

How the profiling advice was useful	Positive responses (%)
Led to the identification of the offender	2.7
Furthered understanding of case/offender	60.9
Expert opinion reassured own judgement	51.6
Offered structure for interviewing	5.4
Other	2.3
Not useful	17.4

Source: Gudjonsson and Copson (1997).

therefore argue that even if police officers say that a profile was useful, that assessment might still flatter to deceive.

Alison *et al.* (2003a) demonstrated this rather convincingly in an experiment. They used an actual profile compiled by an FBI agent. They had a group of senior police officers (n=33, average age=42), and a group of forensic experts (n=30, average age=39) assess this profile that was generated during the investigation of a murder of a young girl. In addition, they provided their participants details of the 'offender' so that the police officers and forensic experts could judge the veracity of the profile (see box for details). In fact however, one group received details of the actual offender, whereas the other group was given bogus details of a very different 'offender'.

Excerpts of the profile used by Alison et al. (2003a)

'The murderer will be a white male between 25 and 35, or the same general age as the victim and of average appearance.'

'The suspect will have difficulty in maintaining any kind of personal relationship with a woman.'

'The sexual acts show controlled aggression, but rage or hatred of women was obviously present.'

'He did not want the woman screaming for help.'

'The murderer's infliction of sexual sadistic acts on an inanimate body suggests he was disorganised.'

'He probably will be a very confused person, possibly with previous mental problems.'

Some surprising findings emerged. Those who received details of the actual murderer found that the profile fitted that person as well as those who received details of a different person altogether! Thus, senior police officers and forensic experts judged the profile to be as accurate in describing an offender who was 19, as a fabricated offender who was 37 years of age. The genuine offender was an unemployed actor with a history of depression and no previous convictions. The fabricated offender had several convictions for burglary and assault and had had various relationships. The actual offender was a stranger, whereas the fabricated one was an acquaintance. Despite all these differences, the experts judged that the profile applied equally well to both. It therefore indeed seems that profiles can be many things to many people, and often very difficult to verify or prove wrong.

In summary, it is clear that profilers hardly ever solve cases on their own accord. But police teams do value the process of consultation and debate with the profiler in the role of independent expert. That dialogue is deemed to be highly useful. Rather than idolising or condemning the quality of offender profiling it makes sense to look at profiling as one of a number of crime analysis techniques. Cope (2005) provides for the following categorisation.

Table 3.6 Crime analysis tools

Technique	Description
Crime pattern analysis	The analysis of patterns of crime, either spatial, linked series or general trends.
Network analysis	The analysis of offenders and their activities and relationships.
Criminal business profile	A profile of the modus operandi of criminal business enterprises.
Market profile	A profile of a crime market, including details of the offenders, geography and assets exchanged.
Operational intelligence assessment	An ongoing review of intelligence throughout an operation.
Target profile	A profile of an individual, including activities and associates.
Results analysis	An assessment of the impact of activity to understand what works to inform decision-making.
Risk analysis	A review of the risks associated with individuals or problems to assess the imperative to intervene.

Source: Cope (2005).

High tech policing. Policing in the twenty-first century is increasingly technology and information driven.
Photo courtesy of Jan Brayley (Hampshire Constabulary).

Conclusion

Psychology is vital in solving crime. That ranges from psychological research on profiling, to the training of police officers on how to interview suspects and witnesses. Furthermore, psychological knowledge of memory, suggestibility and of scripts and schemas have changed the way witness testimony is considered. Such findings help improve criminal investigations and the product of those investigations can change the shape of a criminal trial.

In the next chapter, we take a number of issues identified here into the courtroom. That will include the quality of witness testimony, in particular eyewitness evidence. In addition, miscarriages of justice, and false and recovered memories will be addressed.

Although police investigation is a topic in its own right, its ultimate validation, at least when a suspect pleads 'not guilty' is in the courtroom where the evidence is presented in front of judge and jury.

South African police recruit. One of the world's biggest policing
challenges – delivering security in South Africa.
*Photo courtesy of Chief Constable Frans Heeres (Midden and West Brabant
Police, the Netherlands).*

Chapter 4

Courtroom psychology

The nature of the criminal trial

When we think of a criminal trial we tend to think of trial by jury. In a jury trial in England and Wales, defendants are tried in front of a jury of twelve ordinary people in a Crown Court. A crown prosecutor presents the evidence for the prosecution. Defence counsel operates on behalf of the defendant. Witnesses are called to give their evidence in person and are under oath. The judge, wearing a robe and a wig acts as referee. The judge decides which pieces of evidence are admissible and instructs the jury on the law and on their role. It is for the jury to decide upon a defendant's guilt. In case of a not guilty verdict the defendant walks free. In case of a guilty verdict the judge decides on the sentence.

Most Crown Courts have the same layout. The judge sits on an elevated platform. In front of the judge is space for recorders and clerks. On the judge's right is the witness box. This is where witnesses appear to give their evidence. The jury is seated to the left of the judge. Behind the recorders is the area for both prosecution and defence lawyers. The defence sit to the left of the judge, closer to the jury and the prosecution, next to the defence closer to the gallery. At the back in the dock is where the defendant or defendants sit. The public gallery is opposite the jury.

A Crown Court can be an intimidating place. Crown Courts are characterised by decorum and deference to authority. The judges as well as the prosecuting and defending lawyers wear wigs. When the judge enters the courtroom all rise. When any individual leaves the courtroom while the court is in session, it is customary to bow to the judge when leaving.

The Crown Court is the ultimate decision making platform. It is here where defendants learn their fate: until the jury have reached a verdict, no one knows whether any defendant will walk out a free person, or whether they will be sent to prison for many years. The jury must only return a guilty verdict when they are convinced beyond reasonable doubt that the defendant is guilty. Jury decisions are meant to be unanimous. Where a jury cannot decide that is called a 'hung jury' which might result in a retrial in front of a new jury. It is also possible for the judge to allow the jury to return a so-called majority verdict. That verdict must be supported by at least ten of the twelve jurors.

The Crown Court trial in front of a jury is perhaps the essence of the justice system in England and Wales. But it is important to realise that most cases are dealt with differently. Most minor crimes can be dealt with by means of a caution, or in a Magistrates' court, where a Magistrate (a single judge) decides on both guilt and, in case of a guilty verdict, also on sentencing. When a defendant pleads guilty there will be no jury trial, regardless of the seriousness of the offence. The court will then only concern itself with deciding on a sentence.

Not proven: a jury verdict unique to Scotland

Scotland has its own criminal justice system which is different from that in England and Wales in several respects. The jury decision is one of those differences. Firstly a jury in Scotland consists of 15 members, not 12 as in England and Wales. And they must choose between three verdicts. These are *guilty* or *not guilty* as is the case south of the Scottish border, and their third option is *not proven*. Both a *not proven* and a *not guilty* verdict result in the acquittal of the defendant. It works by majority verdict, so that if 8 of the 15 jurors judge a defendant to be guilty, a guilty verdict is returned (Pakes 2004).

The area of psychology that investigates the goings on at a trial is called *courtroom psychology*. We can identify the following areas. The first is *jury decision making*. The jury decision making process has two components. The first refers to how jurors make up their mind individually. The second is the group process to arrive at a joint decision. Psychologists have extensively studied both processes (e.g. Hastie 1993).

In addition there is a wealth of research that aims to establish how jurors respond to certain types of *evidence*. That includes jurors' understanding of complex scientific evidence, and the extent to which juries understand the law they need to apply in reaching their verdict.

Child witnesses: reducing the risk of trauma

In 1992, England and Wales began to allow videotaped evidence of child sexual assault victims taken from interviews with police and social workers to be used as evidence in chief. An evaluation of the first two years with the new system suggested no impact on conviction rates compared with the previous system (Davies 1999). It does reduce levels of stress and trauma experienced by the child witness.

Ross *et al.* (1994) conducted a study to examine the extent to which protective shields and testimony on video testimony affected the weight attached to the testimony of a child. They found that when participants watched a tape of a sexual abuse trial involving a ten-year old witness as the first witness, conviction rates differed according to how the evidence was given. However, participants who watched the video of the trial in full did not differ in how they judged the case as a whole.

Confident that children can give evidence competently without having to be physically exposed to the intimidating courtroom in England and Wales, so-called 'Special Measures' have been introduced to allow for vulnerable and intimidated witnesses to give evidence in a less confrontational manner as part of an initiative called *Speaking up for Justice* (Home Office 1998). Some of these measures had already been available to children but have since become much more widely in use. They include

- screens – to ensure that the witness does not see the defendant;
- video recorded evidence-in-chief – allowing an interview with the witness, which has been video recorded before the trial, to be shown as the witness's evidence-in-chief in court;
- live link – live television link (CCTV) or other arrangement allowing a witness to give evidence from outside the courtroom;
- clearing the public gallery of the court – so that evidence can be given in private;
- removal of wigs and gowns in court (Home Office 1998).

In 2006 the measures were positively evaluated. Many of these are now standard practice in courtrooms throughout England and Wales.

The value of *eyewitness testimony* is a special case. It is intensely studied whether juries are able to properly weigh eyewitness testimony. Mistaken identification is a major source of miscarriages of justice, alongside false confessions and faulty (or misunderstood) scientific evidence presented by expert witnesses (Huff *et al.* 1996). In addition, we discuss false and recovered memories to assess how jurors evaluate those types of evidence.

Another area of inquiry is that of the impact of so-called *extra-legal factors*. This is information that is not evidence in its own right but might influence a jury anyhow. This includes a defendant's appearance or demeanour, and the persuasion applied by prosecution and defence.

Psychologist in profile

'There are important ethical dimensions to my role'

Andrew Bates
Chartered Forensic Psychologist
Thames Valley Probation Service

'I studied psychology in Exeter and soon after that I started working as a prison psychologist. My MSc degree was Birkbeck's MSc in Applied Criminological Psychology which was the first of its kind in the UK. I then made the shift to community work. I am currently employed by Thames Valley Probation Service. I was involved with an organisation called NOTA, a multi-disciplinary organisation dedicated to work with sexual abusers. Through this organisation I knew many practitioners who were not psychologists and was asked to join the probation service as a forensic psychologist.

Within the probation service a lot of work is done with offenders, including sex offenders in the community. There are many programmes that are accredited, which means that they have been thoroughly evaluated and proven to be able to reduce reoffending. Probation officers often run those programmes. However, there are always complicated cases: people who fall in between services. Offenders can have a variety of needs or disabilities and for that reason, taking part in group programmes might not be suitable for them.

As a forensic psychologist within probation, I tend to focus on the complicated fringes of offender work. I interpret psychometric tests as part of my assessment. That involves issues of risk, deciding on suitable treatment and I also liaise with other professionals, such as psychiatrists, GPs, social workers and the police. These people may not always know exactly what forensic psychology is about and what forensic psychologists can and cannot do. That makes my role a bit ambassadorial: I do not only provide my opinion as a psychologist but I also represent my profession. It is important to get that right.

Probation work used to be mostly social work, supporting the offender. But probation has changed and is much more focused on public protection. That has repercussions for my job. For instance, there might be a situation where the police want to gain a so-called Sex Offence Prevention Order. That way, a judge can forbid a sex offender to go to a park, for example, or to be in direct contact with children. I might testify in court to support such an order. That brings an important ethical dimension to my role. Such orders infringe the liberty of the individual. You therefore have to always ask yourself whether it is necessary. You need to balance the rights of the offender with the interests of society.

Working in probation is interesting and rewarding and working with many other agencies is something I enjoy. I particularly enjoy the most complicated cases. When offenders present with a very complicated profile it is a real challenge to devise a treatment programme that can work. I am fortunate that I work in an environment in which I can make a difference. The people I work with value my opinion and I feel that my training and experience can make a real difference in reducing crime and making society safer.'

Jury decision making

Consider the task of a jury. They are twelve people from all walks of life who have not met before. They are not legally trained and have no specific qualifications. Yet, they will make a decision that will be life changing for the defendant. In the US, unlike in Britain, juries can even decide on the death penalty, so that their decisions are not so much life changing, but possibly even about life or death. That is an enormous responsibility.

The fact that much information is contested and uncertain adds to the jury's burden. Jurors often deal with information that is inconsistent. Prosecution and defence will present different versions of events and contrasting portrayals of the people involved. The jury might hear expert testimony on the chemical composition of drugs, or on the value of DNA evidence. In addition, the information is principally given verbally, through question and answer sessions in examinations and cross-examinations. That is a lengthy process with many trials taking a week or longer. That altogether provides the jury with quite an awesome decision making challenge.

Studying jury decision making

Due the importance of their task, the law seeks to protect jurors from undue influence. One of these protective measures is that their names cannot be revealed in the media. Another is that jury verdicts do not need to be explained or justified. Furthermore, jurors are not allowed to discuss the case or the deliberation process, and finally, it is forbidden for anyone to attend jury deliberations. These restrictions, in place to make sure that the jury is left in peace to reach a verdict, make it impossible to study jury decision making directly, at least in the UK. That is why several alternative methods have been developed to gain insight into jury decision making. These are the use of 'mock juries', 'shadow juries' and research that looks at the decision making of individual jurors. As jurors can be people between 18 and 70 years of age, and from all walks of life, experiments can involve regular participants who can be exposed to various types of evidence.

Mock juries

Mock juries consist of individuals who consider a contrived case. Participants, often university students, are usually presented with a summarised case, often in a written format or on video. This method carries a number of disadvantages. Firstly, the format of the information is rather unlike information at trial. Secondly, the mock jury setting usually has little of the gravitas and decorum of a real-life courtroom setting. Thirdly, mock jurors know that their decision is relatively inconsequential, unlike real juries. Fourthly, the questions that mock juries are asked to answer are often not the same questions asked of real juries, but include judgements on believability, attractiveness, and judging guilt via alternative means such as via 5-point Likert scales.

The main advantage of this method is experimental control. By means of mock juries sensitive issues can be investigated to inform the criminal justice system on their possible effects. One such factor is the issue of race. Sommers (2006) examined the effect of racial composition upon jury decision making among US jurors (see Key study). Sommers argued that for such research questions, a mock jury design is a 'realistic and engaging means for examining group decision making' (Sommers 2006: 597).

Special powers. Much evidence presented in court comes from the police.
Photo courtesy of Jan Brayley (Hampshire Constabulary).

Key study: Racial diversity and jury decision making

On racial diversity and group decision making: Identifying multiple effects of racial composition on jury deliberations

Aim
To examine whether a racially diverse jury deliberates differently from an all white jury.

Method
Participants
All 200 participants were jury eligible citizens from the US state of Michigan.

Method
Participants were shown the trial (a summary of 30 minutes from *Court TV*) of a black defendant and the decision making of racially heterogeneous (four white, two black) was compared with that of racially homogeneous (all white) six-person mock juries.

Results
The analysis comprised both jurors' views prior to deliberation and afterwards. Before even entering deliberations, the white jurors who knew they were going to discuss the case in an all white jury were more convinced of the defendants guilt than those getting ready to deliberate in a mixed jury.

After deliberations, out of the 29 groups 16 reached a unanimous *not guilty* verdict. The key finding was that diverse groups discussed the case more fully. Racially mixed groups deliberated longer, discussed more facts, showed fewer misunderstandings of the facts, and discussed the issue of racism more frequently.

The interesting point was that the difference between all-white and mixed groups was not brought about by the black jurors in the mixed groups. Instead, white jurors in a mixed jury behaved differently from white jurors in an all white jury.

Discussion
Sommers argues that 'this study identifies specific advantages of racial heterogeneity for group decision making' (2006: 609). It seems that a racially diverse jury might simply be a better jury, at least in certain cases. As a racially diverse jury in the UK is not a right (the composition of the jury is by and large 'pot luck' for defendants), that is an intriguing finding.

Source: Sommers (2006).

Shadow juries

Shadow juries are exposed to an actual trial. They are a group of participants recruited to attend proceedings from the public gallery in court and are asked to either deliberate or answer a series of questions afterwards. The advantage of this method is that the information presented is authentic. On the other hand, the decision reached by shadow jurors is still not of the same impact as that faced by the actual jury.

McCabe and Purves (1974) exposed shadow juries to 30 trials in the Oxford Crown court and actually found shadow juries to be slightly more inclined to convict than real juries, which suggests that what real juries do is not identical to the decision making of shadow juries. What is also lost is experimental control. The researcher can select a trial, but cannot manipulate it in any way. Thus, there is more *ecological validity*, but no actual manipulation of the independent variable.

Group processes in jury decision making

Hastie *et al.* (1983) argued that juries generally come to a verdict in three stages. The first is a group process of open-ended 'orientation'. The facts are explored and differences in opinion may be uncovered. Factions may develop. That brings about the second phase, which is called 'open conflict'. In this phase the focus is on debating the evidence in detail and the different interpretations possible. There might be polarised views and heated exchanges. After that, either the jury comes to agreement and returns a verdict, or pressure is applied on those in the minority. It is well known that social pressure is a powerful tool in making people change their decision. The third phase is one of reconciliation in which differences are talked down and individuals praise each other on their input.

The research by Asch (1956) who had participants judge the length of simple straight lines must be borne in mind. If participants could be persuaded to give a blatantly wrong answer due to social pressure, then social pressure could be even more powerful in jury deliberation situations where the truth is ultimately uncertain. Psychological research on group conformity should make us wary of the quality of jury decision-making. The phenomenon of *Groupthink* (Janis 1972) has been applied to such situations. It refers to decision making in closed environments in high stake situations. In such situations, a desire to enhance group cohesion can be such that dissenting views are not voiced. That mindset can bring about extreme decisions, sometimes referred to as the 'risky shift'.

Groupthink

Groupthink tends to occur in highly cohesive groups under pressure. When there is pressure to all agree on a course of action, decisions can occur hastily without due regard for the risks and consequences of the decision. The desire to achieve unanimity can be so intense that doubts are not voiced and alternative options insufficiently explored. It can lead to a phenomenon called the 'risky shift'; situations in which such groups take high-risk, high-stakes decisions. Groupthink can be overcome with strong impartial leadership, the valuing of diversity and dissenting viewpoints. Groups might appoint a 'devil's advocate' whose role it is to constantly challenge the prevailing viewpoint.

On the other hand, the minority can sometimes make the difference and change the mind of the majority. Moscovici *et al.*'s (1969) famous experiment involving blue and green slides demonstrated that a minority of two has a chance of convincing the majority. They are most likely to be successful if they are consistent and do not waver; if it seems that they make a sacrifice while they hold on to their views; are acting on principle, and are seen to be reasonable and flexible, rather than stubborn and obstructive. Thus, it is their consistent behavioural style that can make minorities influential.

Hastie *et al.* (1983) also found that when the verdict has to be unanimous juries tend to be more consensus oriented. They spend more time discussing the case and less time on voting. Juries that can give a majority verdict adopt a more forceful and persuasive style in which the phase of reconciliation often does not occur once the sufficient majority is reached.

Eyewitness testimony

Activity

Imagine that you are a juror in a criminal trial involving an alleged robbery. Say that a corner shop was robbed by an individual carrying a gun and wearing a 'hoodie' as well as dark sunglasses. The key witness is the shopkeeper who was obviously terrified at the time. The shopkeeper gave a description of the assailant to the police. He estimated that the robber was about 20 years old, of medium build and height, wearing jeans, trainers and a dark jacket.

> Now imagine that the police have apprehended a suspect. They have arrested an individual on suspicion of another robbery and are now investigating whether this suspect may have been involved with our corner shop robbery as well. The shopkeeper is asked to come in for an identification in a line-up.
>
> As a group exercise, consider as many factors as possible that can complicate or facilitate recognition.

In the first instance, eyewitness testimony may not seem all that difficult. After all, people are highly adept at face recognition and researchers as early as Charles Darwin in the nineteenth century have argued the importance of recognising familiar faces and reading their facial expression so as to judge their emotions. But eyewitnesses do not always get it right. They can either fail to recognise a perpetrator in a line-up (or from a photograph or video footage), or they point the finger to the wrong person. Both are not rare occurrences.

Fisher and Reardon (2007) mention the fact that the first 40 cases where DNA evidence actually exonerated a convicted person, in 90 per cent of cases mistaken identification was involved. The factors that impinge on a witness correctly identifying a perpetrator can be grouped into *estimator* and *system variables* (Wells 1978). Estimator variables are those factors that are beyond our control. These include the lighting during the event and the length of time that a witness was able to witness the perpetrator. The other group of factors are called system variables. They are, at least in theory, under the control of the police and courts. These factors include how the interview and the line-up was conducted, for instance. Kapardis (2003) groups these factors into four categories. These are, factors to do with

Table 4.1 Variables that can impact on the reliability of eyewitness testimony

Category	Variables
Event	Type of event, lighting, presence of weapon, duration
Witness	Age, ethnicity, alcohol, schemas/stereotypes, victim or not
Perpetrator	Ethnicity, posture, gait, disguise or not
Interrogational	Time between event and testimony, leading questions, post-event misinformation, cognitive interview

Source: Wells and Olsen (2003).

the event; the witness, the perpetrator, and finally, interrogational factors. Only interrogational factors are under the control of the criminal justice system.

The event, the witness and the perpetrator

Estimator variables comprise event, witness and perpetrator variables. Event variables include their duration. Clifford and Richards (1977) conducted a study in which police officers had either a 15 second or a 30 second conversation with an individual. The researchers found that these police officers were better able to recognise the individuals with whom they spoke longer. Wagenaar and Van der Schrier (1994) investigated the effect of lighting and the distance between witness and perpetrator on later recognition. They found that if the event occurs in the dark and the perpetrator is more than 15 metres away from the witness, subsequent recognition in broad daylight will be severely hampered.

A particular factor to do with the crime situation is the presence of a weapon. Its presence grabs the attention of many witnesses and therefore distracts them from observing the face or other features of the offender. This is called 'weapon focus' (Loftus *et al.* 1987).

Selective attention

The weapon focus effect, when a witness focuses primarily on the weapon in a situation is a particular form of selective attention. Selective attention impacts on memory, as the information that is not attended to is much less likely to enter *working memory* and to be stored in *long-term memory*. The weapon is for obvious reasons highly salient and that will affect recall of most other information from that situation.

It has been found that both the elderly and very young children sometimes perform worse than regular adults. They are no worse when they are shown a line-up and the perpetrator is actually present: both the elderly and very young children are quite capable of a correct identification in such circumstances. In the absence of the perpetrator, when the correct answer is that 'they are not there', both young children and the elderly are more likely to incorrectly identify someone else in the line-up as the culprit.

There are a number of witness factors that can influence their ability to recognise a perpetrator at a later stage. Meissner and Brigham (2001) found that race was an issue in eyewitness identification. It is not that certain ethnic groups are better or worse in recognising perpetrators in a line-up, but it seems easier to recognise individuals of our own ethnic group than others.

When examining perpetrator factors it has been found that a highly distinctive face is more easily recognised and disguises make recognition more difficult. The same is true in cases where the perpetrator wore sunglasses but Hockley *et al.* (1999) found that that is less problematic when the perpetrator also wears sunglasses in the line-up.

Many of these factors are perhaps common knowledge. Jurors do not need to be told that if a witness only saw the perpetrator for a brief moment, in the dark and from a distance, that any recognition must be taken with a pinch of salt. Other factors however, might not be so self-explanatory. One of these might be the certainty with which a witness identifies a person. A highly confident and absolutely certain witness is more likely to be persuasive than a hesitant witness who is not altogether sure. However, there is a great deal of research that highlights that those who are most certain in their recognition are not more often correct than those who are more hesitant (Deffenbacher 1980). That is possibly a factor about which jurors should be told.

Interrogation or system variables

We saw in the previous chapter that oppressive police questioning can lead vulnerable suspects to confess to crimes they never committed. It is even possible for some of these suspects to honestly come to believe that they committed that crime. What is true for suspects is true for witnesses as well: the way in which they are instructed will to a significant degree determine the quality of their evidence. These factors are interrogation or system variables.

System variables are to do with retrieval. Imagine that you witnessed the commission of crime. You saw the perpetrator, but were not able to observe him for very long. You were interviewed by the police and you provided a description of the offender. A few weeks later you are again contacted by the police. They want you to do an identification.

You might be inclined to assume that the police caught the offender. They would not ask you to come if there was no suspect, you might assume. Thus, when you look at the line-up, you may well be convinced that the offender is present. That is in fact what many witnesses think. They reason that the police would not be wasting their and everybody else's time by constructing a line-up without the person who they think is the perpetrator. This has consequences for the task that witnesses face.

Wells (1984) conducted a study in which eyewitnesses were exposed to a line-up of five individuals, but from which the actual offender was absent. Amazingly, 68 per cent identified another person as the offender! They simply pointed to the person who, to their mind, most closely resembled that actual offender. It shows the power of the assumption that the actual offender 'must be there'. The police therefore emphasise to the witness that the offender 'may or may not' be present in the line-up. Steblay (1997) found that such an instruction considerably reduced the likelihood of witnesses making an incorrect identification.

A further factor that impacts on witnesses' performance in eyewitness identification is to do with the decoys. Also referred to as 'fillers', these are the people that make up the numbers but are not suspects. They must be sufficiently similar to the suspect so that the suspect does not automatically stand out. The police usually use witness descriptions to select these decoys, to make sure that the suspect is surrounded by suitable alternatives that a witness may choose from. All persons in the line-up may be asked to wear a hat, or sunglasses, depending on the circumstances in which the witness initially saw the offender.

Finally, a further method to ensure that the witness will only point to the person they actually recognise is the so-called *sequential line-up*. That means that the witness is exposed to the members of the line-up one by one. Whenever the witness decides that 'that's him (or her)' the process is halted. That stops the witness simply picking the person who resembles the offender most, without actually recognising them. Steblay *et al.* (2001) found that a sequential line reduces the number of incorrect identifications by half. Unfortunately, it also slightly decreased the number of correct identifications. This is perhaps because this technique makes witnesses slightly more conservative: they will only identify if they are certain, whereas they perhaps would identify in a traditional line-up, due to demand characteristics (they assume that the offender 'must be there'), and because one individual in the line actually rather resembles their memory of the offender. A sequential line-up is likely to reduce these demand characteristics.

Wells and Olsen argue that to conduct a proper line-up is rather like constructing a psychological experiment on perception and memory. There is a hypothesis to be tested, i.e. the suspect is guilty. An experiment is designed to test that, which is the line up procedure. As in any study, the set-up might be biased, witnesses might suffer from demand characteristics, and those conducting the line-up might be unwittingly influencing the

Say what? Ear witness testimony

A witness may not have seen a crime taking place, but instead may have overheard a conversation. With eyewitnesses, the police conduct a line-up and similarly, we could construct a voice line-up to decide whether the voice heard by a witness belongs to the perpetrator. How good are people at recognising voices?

People are better at recognising a voice speaking their own language than another language. In addition, ear witnesses are more accurate in target-present line-ups than in target-absent line-ups (Philippon *et al.* 2007). The same was found for eyewitnesses.

Kerstholt *et al.* (2006) examined the effect of three variables on ear witness performance. The first was retention interval, the time between hearing the voice and having to recognise it from a line-up. The second was the effect of local accent: is a person with a standard accent more easily recognised than someone with a strong regional accent? The third variable was whether a voice line-up by telephone would be as effective as a voice line-up via tape. As phone transmissions lack naturalness and timbre it is worth testing whether that affects recognition.

Participants heard a standard accented or a regionally accented voice over the phone or on tape. The target (the correct voice) was either absent or present in the subsequent line-up, and could be over the phone or via a tape. Finally, the line-up could take place either three or eight weeks after the voice was originally heard.

The first finding is that voice recognition is not easy. In target-absent line-ups, only 28 per cent of participants confirmed that the actual voice they heard was not there. A majority said that they weren't sure or picked out the wrong voice. In the target-present line-ups, only 24 per cent picked the right voice.

Participants did find the standard accent voice easier to recognise. In addition, there was an interesting effect of retention rate. You would expect that the longer the time between hearing the voice and recognition, the more difficult the task becomes. But in the target-absent line-up, performance actually improved: after a longer period, participants seemed happier to say that the voice 'was not there'.

There was no effect of telephone. Performance did not change regardless of whether they initially heard the voice over the phone, or whether their line-up was via the telephone. That can have relevance for the organisation of such line-ups by the police as use of the telephone has considerable practical advantages.

witness (that would be an experimenter effect). The best line-ups would be those that involve so-called *double blind testing*, where both the witness and the person conducting the line-up do not know who the supposed culprit is. That removes the opportunity for the experimenter to subconsciously influence the witness. In line-up research and in police practice, that, unfortunately is a rarity (Wells and Olson 2003).

In summary, the issue is not that eyewitness testimony is not perfect. Most evidence at trial is, in one way or another uncertain and part of the jury's task is to reach a verdict taking that into account. However, it is potentially dangerous if juries were to assume that eyewitness testimony is fail proof whereas in fact research has established that it is not. Therefore, the police follow so-called ADVOKATE guidelines to reduce the likelihood of that happening.

Judging eyewitness accounts properly: ADVOKATE

ADVOKATE is an acronym. It is a mnemonic tool for those assessing eyewitness accounts to ensure that it is properly weighed (e.g., Kebbell and Wagstaff 1999). Guidelines from the National Crime Faculty stipulated that these factors must be addressed and recorded as part of eyewitness statements (National Crime Faculty 1998).

Amount of time under observation
Distance from the eyewitness to the person/incident
Visibility
Obstructions to view
Known or seen before
Any reason to remember
Time lapse
Errors or material discrepancies

This set of guidelines is known as the Turnbull rules, as they were specified in the case against Turnbull and others in 1977 (*R v Turnbull 1977*). It is a demonstration that psychological knowledge can change legal and police practice.

False or recovered memories

A good decade ago, the issues of false versus recovered memories was a hotly debated issue in criminal psychology. An important one as well: hundreds of individuals, usually after therapy reported the existence of memories of often horrific, childhood sexual abuse. Prior to therapy, they had no recollection of such events but during therapy sessions often involving hypnosis the memories resurfaced. Several cases involving recovered memories made it to court in the US. George Franklin famously got convicted on the basis of recovered memory testimony although the verdict was later overturned (Loftus and Ketcham 1994).

The mechanism to cause 'forgetting' of traumatic events is assumed to be repression. The concept of repression has a long history in psychology with Freud postulating it as a way in which the mind copes with traumatic experiences. But its validity, even its very existence has been questioned by psychologists (e.g. Loftus 1993). They claim that most, or even all 'recovered memories' are false. They worry about the fact that innocent individuals would be sent to prison on the basis of such evidence and that therapists who 'plant' false memories do a great deal of harm.

There are two empirical questions that we can derive from this. The first is: can highly painful and traumatic events be entirely forgotten, and at some point, many years later, be correctly remembered? The second is: is it possible to plant 'memories' in a person's head that are actually entirely made up? The debate is complex and strikes at the heart of the nature of memory and the reliability of testimony. A full discussion is beyond the scope of this book, but it is important to provide evidence for each proposition. We leave it up to you to decide which side makes the best case.

Can people come to believe events happened to them that never occurred at all? The short answer is, yes, they can. Many people believe they have been abducted by aliens, and many people report memories of biologically or physically impossible events (Wright *et al.* 2006). The planting of fake memories has also been established via psychological experiments. Suggestive questions and misleading information seem to be able to do the trick. The classic study is that of Loftus and Pickrell (1995). It is about planting a false memory of being lost in a shopping mall (shopping centre) at five years old. There were 24 participants who each brought a relative. These participants were given three anecdotes about their youth, two were true (provided by the relative) and one was made up and the relative was there to make sure that that story was both credible and entirely false.

Participants would then be asked whether they recall any of these events and to discuss their memories. About two-thirds of true events were recalled and initially, one in four actually claimed some recollection of the fake event. After two interviews their memories had 'become' clearer and more vivid. At the end, when all were explained that two memories were real and one was fake, one in five decided that the fake memory must be real and picked one of the true memories to be false. It shows that planting false memories, at least about events such as this, can be done. That of course does not prove that you could implant highly traumatic memories as easily, but it does highlight the constructive nature of memory. It of course does not prove that false memories do not exist.

How can you tell that a memory is recovered? For that it needs to refer to a true event; it must have been forgotten for some time, and then accurately recovered. That is difficult to assess. As recovered memories often involve childhood events of many years ago, independent verification is often difficult, especially if they concern secretive events such as incest. Secondly, it is difficult to establish whether a memory is repressed, or whether a person simply has learnt to not think about it. Finally, it is not easy to establish whether the memory is actually accurate. Therefore, cases of proclaimed recovered memory (e.g. Cheit 2005) require careful scrutiny. That said, even when individual cases of recovered memories would be found to be untrue, that does not mean that recovered memories do not exist. The debate continues.

Extra-legal factors

It is true to say that the outcome of some trials hinges on more than evidence alone. That is a concern. After all, we want defendants to be tried fairly and the decision based on nothing but the evidence. When other factors come into play they can introduce an element of unfairness. In this section we shall examine two extra-legal factors, the attractiveness of the defendant and the extent to which jurors are swayed by persuasion rather than by evidence. Apart from that we will also look at attractiveness, persuasion, the effect of stereotypes and the role of 'believing in a just world'.

Attractiveness

Being good looking is an advantage in life. People judge attractive people to be more honest, competent and trustworthy. Mobius and Rosenblat (2006) call this the *physical attractiveness stereotype*. It is also referred to as an instance of the 'Halo effect' (Thorndike 1920). Often summarised under the catchphrase 'beauty is good' is has been demonstrated that beauty is perceived to be linked with intelligence, social skills, health and sexual prowess, and these are just a few of the positive attributes bestowed upon physically attractive people. It is therefore no wonder that attractiveness has been researched in courtroom situations as well.

Efran (1974) conducted an early study on the influence of attractiveness of the defendant. He showed participants a photo of a female student who was accused of cheating. The attractiveness of the student was varied to assess whether her attractiveness affected other students' judgements on her guilt and the penalty that she should receive. Efran found that male students were affected but female students were not.

Sigall and Ostrove (1975) demonstrated that attractiveness does not always work in a defendant's favour. They found that an attractive female burglar would be sentenced more leniently than an unattractive burglar, but when the crime is such that attractiveness might facilitate it, such as deception, then the effect disappears. Thus, there are scenarios conceivable in which being attractive is not an advantage, when jurors might conclude that the defendant used their good looks to commit the crime in the first place.

Both studies utilised artificial materials and settings. Therefore their ecological validity can be questioned. Bull and McAlpine warned about the risk of generalising 'from simple-minded simulations to the real world' (Bull and McAlpine 1998: 71). Stewart (1980) had a team of observers attend criminal trials, and concluded that attractiveness did not bear upon decisions of guilt, but could have an impact on sentencing. Thus, overall, there might be some effect of attractiveness, but it may well be moderated by many other courtroom and evidential factors.

Stereotypes

Gross (2005) describes stereotypes as Implicit Personality Theories. The process of stereotyping involves three steps. Firstly, we assign someone to a particular group. In our case that could be 'sex offender'. Subsequently we bring into play the belief that all members of this group share certain characteristics (the stereotype). In our case that might be that all sex offenders are evil monsters who prey on innocent victims under the cover of darkness. Thirdly, we infer that the individual in question must also possess these qualities.

Persuasion in the courtroom

There are plenty of efforts to persuade the jury in a criminal trial. The very nature of persuasion suggests that it is a matter of style over substance: jurors are expected to be sensitive to the way in which information is presented rather than to the evidence in its own right.

Pennington and Hastie (1992, 1993) explain that jurors do not weigh pieces of evidence separately. Instead, they impose a narrative organisation on the material, and then judge to what extent the evidence fits that story. The story is the glue that holds the evidence together. Evidence that does not fit the story will be given less weight whereas evidence that supports it will strengthen the juror's conviction.

Because of the story-making process, the order in which evidence is presented can be of influence. Pennington and Hastie found that evidence presented in story order was judged to be more compelling than evidence in a different order. What makes a good story? A story is judged to be good if it has high coverage. That means that it fits (covers) most of the evidence presented. In addition, a story must be coherent, and that means that it must be plausible, consistent and complete. When a story is constructed and judged to be good in terms of coverage and coherence, the juror selects the verdict that fits the story (Pennington and Hastie 1993).

Stereotypes

MacLin and Herrera from the University of El Paso in the US conducted a study on criminal stereotypes (MacLin and Herrera 2006). They devised a Criminal Stereotype Questionnaire (CSQ) which assesses students' ideas about criminals. The questionnaire asked various open-ended questions about the students' images when thinking about criminals including their likely profession, age, personality and appearance. To give you a flavour of the results, the top eight frequently provided characteristics for criminal hair were: short, black, dark, messy, bald, long, brown, and dirty, comprising 77 per cent of total responses. The top 14 most frequently provided responses for criminal clothing were: jeans, baggy clothes, black clothing, t-shirts, cap/hat, old clothing, jumpsuit/jail uniform, ski mask, sleeveless shirt, tennis shoes, white shirt, suits, boots and a jacket. The number one physical characteristic associated with criminals was the presence of tattoos.

The researchers also found that the personality traits that were believed to be common among criminals were sociability (35 per cent), vindictiveness (14 per cent), being introverted (13 per cent), being angry (6 per cent), and being antisocial (6 per cent). It is interesting that introverted is mentioned as the empirical evidence actually suggests that the opposite might be the case. Overall, a typical criminal is perceived to be tall, with long or shaggy dark hair, wears baggy, dirty and/or dark clothing, may have some form of facial hair, and beady eyes. Skin features associated with criminals are scars and pock marks.

In order to interpret these findings, we must realise that the sample here involved American students who were overwhelmingly (close to 90 per cent) Hispanic. It is conceivable that a different sample of respondents would demonstrate a slightly different stereotype. The implications of this finding are nevertheless stark. Any suspect or defendant may more or less correspond to such a stereotype. That brings about the risk that such stereotypes might influence decision making in their cases.

In the next chapter we will examine research involving stereotypes and death penalty decisions which demonstrates that racial stereotypes may indeed be a factor in sentencing.

Believing in a just world

The so-called 'just world' hypothesis is an important phenomenon for courtroom psychology. It suggests that people have a need to assume that their world is orderly, predictable and fair. Such an outlook may make the world less threatening and information that challenges that reassuring view is therefore uncomfortable. Jury trials often provide that kind of information: an innocent person is allegedly victimised and that challenges our assumption that mostly, you get what you deserve in life.

Jurors might therefore have a tendency of blaming the victim (Lerner 1980). Their reasoning would be that if something horrible happens to the individual they somehow must have brought that upon themselves. Former England footballer and national manager Glenn Hoddle showed the strength of his belief in a just world (as well as in reincarnation) when he stated that people with a disability were punished for wrongdoings in an earlier life, in a newspaper interview in 1999. It cost him his job.

It has been demonstrated that individuals with a strong attachment to their belief that the world is a just place and people get what they deserve are less sympathetic to rape victim accounts: i.e. 'she must, somehow, have deserved it'.

In conclusion, jurors bring a great number of personal attributes into the courtroom. Some might work against the defendant, such as their demeanour, or whether their appearance fits a 'criminal stereotype'. On the other hand, a juror's belief in a just world might just work in a defendant's favour, as would their tendency to acquit in case of doubt.

Jury deliberation can be equally advantageous or otherwise to the fate of defendants. In many deliberations, jurors are torn between conformity and independence, between persuasion and resisting persuasion. A hung jury works in the defendant's favour. But then a majority verdict might push through a guilty verdict despite dissenting opinions. All these factors combined make jury trials rather unpredictable. That is perhaps as much an asset as it is a liability.

Crime prevention. ... with a twist! Spikey, a device to stop drinks from being spiked with drugs
Photo courtesy of R&G Products.

Miscarriages of justice

What if justice gets it wrong? When innocent individuals are wrongfully convicted we speak of a *miscarriage of justice*. In England and Wales there have been a number of high profile instances. We describe the *Cardiff Three* in a separate box. Perhaps the most famous miscarriages of justice are two that had to do with Irish terrorism. Gerald Conlon, Paul Hill, Carole Richardson and Patrick Armstrong become known as the *Guildford Four*. They were convicted for the murder of five people by bombing the Horse and Groom public house in Guildford in 1974. Their convictions were quashed in 1989. Hugh Callaghan, Patrick Hill, Gerry Hunter, Richard McIlkenny, Billy Power and Johnny Walker are collectively known as the *Birmingham Six*. They were convicted of a bombing of two pubs, both in Birmingham, that killed 21 people. Their convictions were quashed in 1991 (Savage and Milne 2007).

Miscarriages of justice strike at the heart of our faith in the criminal justice system. So how do they come about and what can be done to prevent them? First we examine research from the US. Gross *et al.* (2005) looked at all official exonerations between 1989 and 2003. They documented 340 cases, 327 men and 13 women. In 144 cases, it was DNA evidence that proved their innocence. On average these individuals had been in prison for over ten years. Some had died in prison and were posthumously cleared of their guilt. Out of these 340 cases, 205 were cases of murder, and 121 were cases of rape or sexual assault. Together that is the overwhelming majority. They also found that for rape cases, mistaken identification is the biggest factor in producing wrongful convictions in the first place. For murders (where there might be no witness) it is false confessions. As false confessions are often associated with oppressive questioning or other forms of police misconduct, it is perhaps not a surprise that Gross *et al.* found frequent evidence of police misconduct in many of these exonerated cases as well. In addition, many wrongful convictions came about because of lies told in court, either by the police, expert witnesses or individuals with a stake in the outcome. All these come under 'perjury' (lying in court) in the table below.

These data show that criminal psychology matters. Eyewitness identification (or rather, mistaken identification) is a major cause of miscarriages of justice. That makes highlighting its error-proneness an important task. The same is true for false confessions and the role of interview techniques in producing false confessions.

Table 4.2 Causes of wrongful convictions

	Murder (n = 205)	Rape (n = 121)
Eyewitness misidentification	50%	88%
Perjury	56%	25%
False confessions	20%	7%

Source: Gross *et al.* (2005).

What can be done about miscarriages of justice?

In England and Wales there is the Criminal Cases Review Commission (CCRC). It is an independent public body set up to investigate possible miscarriages of justice in England, Wales and Northern Ireland. The Commission assesses whether convictions or sentences should be referred to a court of appeal for reconsideration. Since its inception in 1997, the CCRC has reviewed almost 8,951 cases. On 31 March 2007, the Commission had referred 356 (4 per cent) cases. Thus, only one in 25 or so

DNA to the rescue: 15 years on

On Valentine's Day 1988 Lynette White was found murdered in Cardiff. She was a prostitute and was stabbed no less then 50 times. The police launched a large investigation and with the help of the BBC's *Crimewatch* five suspects, all local men were arrested. The case went to Swansea Crown Court in November 1988. Three of the men, Steven Miller, Yusef Abdullahi and Tony Paris, were found guilty and sentenced to life imprisonment. Steven Miller was Lynette's boyfriend and pimp, and at trial much was made of a confession obtained from him. However, an Appeal's Judge ruled that a miscarriage of justice had taken place. The police interrogation had been deemed to be inappropriate. The Cardiff Three were freed two years after their conviction. For years, the actual killer remained at large.

Years later, in 2000, the police found traces of blood behind a layer of paint on a skirting board, in the room were Lynette Whyte had been murdererd twelve years earlier. A DNA profile was taken. All five original suspects voluntarily provided DNA samples and it was concluded that the blood on the skirting board at the murder scene was not theirs.

In addition, the sample was run through the National DNA Database. But it failed to yield an exact match. However, one component of the DNA from the blood on the skirting board was quite a rare component, and a sample was run on that component alone. It yielded 600 matches. Most of those individuals could easily be ruled out and that left a sample of 70 people. One boy actually matched very closely but he was not even born at the time of the offence. However, it led the police to ask the boy's family to submit samples for analysis. They did, and one family member in fact produced a perfect match. This was how, 15 years after the offence, the actual killer, Jeffrey Gafoor was identified. He was sentenced to life imprisonment in 2003.

Source: BBC News (2005).

cases that are referred to the commission are actually forwarded to an appeals court. However, once that happens, in some two out of three cases the conviction is quashed, and the individual no longer found guilty. Thus, both in the US and in the UK there are procedures by which convictions that are deemed unsafe can be reconsidered and where appropriate undone. The damage to the individuals involved can be mitigated by compensation, but the time spent languishing in a prison cell can never fully be compensated.

Research into miscarriages of justice has been invigorated by the realisation that wrongful convictions are not the only type of miscarriages of justice. A failure to convict an obviously guilty person is equally a travesty (Savage and Milne 2007). The criminal justice system should equally strive to prevent the occurrence of such events. The most notable miscarriage of justice of the 'failure to convict' type is seen by many as the racist murder of teenager Stephen Lawrence. The failure to convict anyone for this crime has damaged public confidence in both the Metropolitan Police as well as the judicial system (Stephen Lawrence Inquiry 1999).

The face of criminal justice. Before a case comes to court, it will have come to a police station first.
Photo courtesy of Jan Brayley (Hampshire Constabulary).

Chapter 5

Sentencing and punishment

In Chapter 1 we saw that there are over 10 million crimes committed in England and Wales each year. Currently the prison system holds just over 80,000 inmates. From comparing those two statistics one conclusion can be drawn: most offenders are not in prison. We have seen that most crimes are never prosecuted. But in addition, community sentences and fines are imposed much more frequently than prison sentences.

In this chapter we shall first examine the process of sentencing. After that we shall look at the implementation of sentences which we call punishment. Punishment is an emotive term. It implies the infliction of harm. Indeed, that is part of the reason why punishment is imposed. But it not the only or even the prevailing reason. Other factors that come into play include *rehabilitation*, which is based on the idea that offenders can be changed, and that those changes will reduce the chance of reoffending. A further consideration is *public protection*. When we take an offender out of the community, that community will no longer be at risk of the offending behaviour of that individual.

Sentencing

Most of the time, a sentence is imposed with several reasons in mind. A judge might send a violent offender to prison because that sentence corresponds to a *tariff*. That means that a prison sentence is the 'going rate' for that offence. In addition, a judge might decide that whilst in prison, the offender should undertake either counselling or training. Such skills might decrease the likelihood of reoffending. Finally, a judge might decide that the needs of the victim are best served with a particular sentence.

Apart from prison a judge has a range of sentencing options. We make a distinction between three types of sentences. The first is prison, or detention, often called *custodial* sentences. The second comprises *community sentences* which most of the time are community orders. They can involve a variety of activities. One of these activities is unpaid work. In 2007 there were about 55,000 instances of unpaid work community orders completed. Other community orders can involve training, taking part in so-called accredited programmes designed to reduce reoffending. They can also involve mental health, alcohol or drugs treatment. Much punishment, therefore, is in fact community based (Ministry of Justice 2008). Finally, the sentence in fact most often handed out is the fine (half of these are for motoring offences). See Table 5.1 below for how often each type of sentence was given in 2006.

Table 5.1 Sentences given in 2006

Type of Sentences	Frequency	%
Custodial (prison)	96,000	8%
Community punishment	190,500	15%
Fine	961,500	77%

Source: Sentencing Statistics (2007).

Sentencing as a human process

There are 77 Crown Court venues in England and Wales. This is the venue where serious cases are tried in front of a jury. In 2006, some 80,000 criminal cases were forwarded to the Crown Court. In a majority of cases (64 per cent) the defendant (or defendants) pleaded guilty. Where an offender pleads 'not guilty' there is a jury trial. In 59 per cent of such cases a defendant is acquitted.

Just like prison is the tip of the iceberg in terms of punishment, so is the Crown Court trial the exception and not the rule. No less than 1.78 million people were proceeded against in Magistrates' courts. These are the lower courts without a jury. Minor offences called *summary offences* are tried here. These are small misdemeanours such as traffic offences. There is also a category of offences called *either way* offences. They include theft and can be tried in a Magistrates' court before a judge or in a Crown Court before judge and jury. The defendant can choose in a case of an *either way* offence in which court the case should be tried. Most choose the lower court, the Magistrates' court as the venue. *Crown Court only* offences are the most serious including murder and rape (Judicial and Court Statistics 2007).

In both Crown Courts and Magistrates' courts the sentence is decided upon by the judge. Any sentence is partly tailored to the offence and in part to the offender. But the fact remains that sentencing is a human process (Hogarth 1971).

Gender and race

Extra-legal factors are factors that are not evidence in their own right but can affect decision making nevertheless. Much studied extra-legal factors include class, gender and race. Kapardis (1985) examined a number of extra-legal factors that can impinge on sentencing in Britain. He found an interesting effect of gender. He reported a study by Wilczynski and Morris (1993) who analysed 474 cases of *infanticide*: where a child of less than one year old had been killed by a parent. They found that female defendants were more likely to be dealt with on the basis of diminished responsibility and were more likely to receive lenient and non-custodial sentences. They concluded that women who kill their own child were perceived as different from men who do the same: 'a woman must have been "mad" to kill her own child' (Wilczynski and Morris, 1993: 36).

In Britain, the impact of race on sentencing is not straightforward. However, Fitzgerald (1994) concluded that there is a small effect at various stages where discrimination might occur and that might have a substantial cumulative effect.

The effect of race in the US is an altogether different matter. That is of particular importance as sentencing in the US is the province of the jury. In addition in many US states the jury has the option (for certain crimes when aggravating circumstances apply) of imposing the death penalty. That makes race and sentencing in the US a poignant area of research.

The news is not good. Simple death penalty trial statistics tell a story. Aguirre and Baker (1993) found that black defendants are five times more likely to be sentenced to death for murder and even nine times more likely to receive the death penalty for rape (see also, Amnesty International 1999).

Baldus and colleagues (Baldus *et al.* 1983, 1990) found existence of both a 'black defendant' and a 'white victim' effect when they examined the practice of the death penalty in the US state of Georgia. The first refers to the fact that black defendants are more likely to receive the death penalty for similar offences than white defendants. In addition, the race of the victim is important: black perpetrators convicted of offending against a white victim are substantially more likely to receive the death penalty than those whose victim is also black. The data is listed in Table 5.2. The odds of receiving the death penalty are worse for black defendants who offended against a white victim (22 per cent of all such cases). Black defendants who offended against a black victim are far less likely to receive the death penalty (only 1 per cent of such cases ended in a death penalty sentence). White defendants receive the death penalty less often overall, and if they do, it is more likely for a crime against a white victim (8 per cent versus 3 per cent).

Table 5.2 Race and the death penalty

Death penalty (%)	Black defendant	White defendant
Black victim	1	3
White victim	22	8

Source: Baldus *et al.* (1990).

Thus, although black defendants are more likely to be sentenced to death overall, there is another effect at play. It seems to add to the disturbing nature of the effect of race on sentencing in the US: the least likely to receive the death penalty are so-called 'black-on-black' offences.

There is in fact research that indicates that this opposite effect, a 'black-on-black leniency' effect has a long history in US criminal justice as well. In 1961 Bullock examined sexual assault cases in the US state of Texas in the 1950s. At first sight the findings are striking: 29 per cent of African Americans received long prison sentences for sexual assault, but no less than 71 per cent of white Americans did (in Texas in 1958). You might have expected the exact opposite as a result of discriminatory practices against black citizens. The answer however lies in examining the race of the victim. Bullock found that crimes that were typically intra-racial, such as murder and sexual assault, were treated differently from typically inter-racial crimes like burglary because 'local norms tolerate a less vigorous enforcement of the law... [when] the disorder is mainly located within the Negro society' (1961: 416). In short, when a black person sexually offends against another black person, at least in 1950s Texas, treatment is more lenient, as if to suggest that crimes among black people are less of a concern to the criminal justice system.

Key study: Looking deathworthy

Looking deathworthy: perceived stereotypicality of black defendants predicts capital-sentencing outcomes

Aim
To establish whether black defendants in the US are more likely to receive the death penalty if their appearance is more stereotypically black.

Method (Phase 1)
The researchers used a database of death penalty eligible cases from Pennsylvania, USA (600 cases from between 1979 and 1999). They selected all black defendants. Their photographs were rated by Stanford undergraduate students on stereotypicality (they were told that they could use any facial feature). They were not told who these men were. This was one factor used to predict whether a death penalty was actually imposed or not (alongside type of crime, victim, etc.).

Results
Defendants who were perceived to be more stereotypically black were more likely to receive the death penalty. Further analysis yielded an interaction effect: stereotypicality was not a factor when both victim and defendant were black. However, when the victim was white, stereotypicality was a factor.

Discussion
Race in sentencing in the US is a controversial factor. This study adds the element of stereotypicality to that. Why is that so? Eberhart *et al.* (2006) argue: 'One possibility is that the interracial character of cases involving a black defendant and a white victim renders race especially salient. Such crimes could be interpreted (…) as matters of intergroup conflict.'

Source: Eberhardt *et al.* (2006).

There is increasing discomfort with the death penalty in the US. Part of that unease is related to issues of race but the main driver has been miscarriages of justice. Mainly thanks to DNA profiling, more and more defendants sentenced to death are in fact found to be innocent. Since 2000 there have been about five exonerations per year (Death Penalty Information Center 2008). Overall, fewer defendants have been put to death in recent years. The peak was 1999 with 98 executions. In contrast, 2006 and 2007 saw 53 and 42 executions, respectively.

Psychologist in profile

'Psychologists regularly speak about their findings in Court'

Mr Martin Fisher
Area Psychologist
HM Prison Service

'I did a joint honours degree in Psychology and Zoology at Manchester Victorian University. As I was not exactly sure what to do next, I applied to become a Civil Servant and started working in the Prison Service. Initially I was posted to Wakefield Prison, a maximum security prison in West Yorkshire. After four years I was posted to HMP Whitemoor in Cambridgeshire. At the time staff got posted and were expected to move to wherever the next posting was. At HMP Whitemoor I worked with sex offenders and "main" prisoners. When I started working in the prison service working with offenders often was on an individual basis but whilst I was at HMP Whitemoor a move to group work became in vogue. In the meantime, I completed an MSc in Applied Criminological Psychology at Birkbeck College in London. I am now a Chartered Forensic Psychologist, Chartered Scientist and Associate fellow of the British Psychological Society.

Four years later I was posted to Albany Prison on the Isle of Wight, and since 2006 my role has been psychologist for the HMPS area of South Central. It means that I oversee the quality of psychological services for 16 prisons in the South of England. A consequence of being promoted to such a position is that one does less clinical work, although I choose to do some. I tend to work on cases of 'high complexity'. That means that what I do will not only be judged by professionals within the criminal justice system, but the public may read about the cases in the newspapers. It is therefore important to present professionally. It would be negative both for myself and for Prison Service Psychology in general, if our work was dismissed as inadequate.

This is why I will often emphasise that psychologists need more than just psychological skills. To know your psychology is not enough. You have to know the prison system and what everyone in it does. You also have to know how bodies like the Parole Board operate. Psychologists regularly speak in front of Parole Boards and other judicial bodies to give their professional opinion. You have to be able to speak with clarity and authority. In addition, your written report must be excellent. Such panels can be unforgiving environments, and therefore it can be highly demanding and stressful. But at the same time, you know that you can make a difference.

A small, but interesting part of my role is Crisis Negotiation work. This comes into effect should there be an incident arising within a prison. It might involve barricades, or, as it were, "rooftop" situations. As a psychologist, I might deploy negotiation advice to negotiators in order to diffuse and resolve situations without any harm to individuals. That might not happen very often, but you never know when the phone will ring and there actually is a crisis!'

Punishment in the UK

Imprisoned in the UK

There are over 80,000 people in Britain's prisons. There are different types of prison such as specific prisons for women, for example Holloway in London. Juveniles are usually kept in Young Offender Institutions (YOIs, such as Feltham in Surrey). Similarly, prison inmates are categorised as well. Newburn describes these four categories.

1 Category A: prisoners whose escape would be highly dangerous to the public, police or security of the state and for whom the aim must be to make escape impossible.
2 Category B: prisoners who do not need the highest conditions of security but for whom escape must be made very difficult.
3 Category C: prisoners who cannot be trusted in open conditions but who do not have the ability or resources to make a determined escape attempt.
4 Category D: prisoners who can reasonably be trusted to serve their sentences in open conditions.

Source: Newburn (2007).

Entering prison. Prisons have special provisions for 'first night' new inmates. They are particularly at risk of suicide and self-harm.
Photo courtesy of Francis Pakes.

A further categorisation system is in place for offenders with severe mental health problems. They can be kept in either high secure units, such as Broadmoor in Berkshire or medium secure units, such as Ravenswood House in Hampshire. In such institutions these individuals can be treated for their illness whilst the public is protected at the same time.

Prisons are not happy places. In 2007 the number of self inflicted deaths was 92. In addition, 80–90 per cent have some, often minor but sometimes very serious, mental health problems (Singleton *et al*. 1998). Furthermore, prisons are the 'home' of the excluded and the unskilled. The government's Social Exclusion Unit summarises that as follows. Prisoners are 13 times more like to have been in care as a child. They are ten times more likely to have been a regular truant. They are 15 times more likely to be HIV positive. In addition, many prisoners are poorly educated and lack basic literacy and numeracy skills. Eighty per cent have the writing skills, 65 per cent the numeracy skills and 50 per cent the reading skills of an 11-year old (Social Exclusion Unit 2002).

The truth is that prison makes many things worse. A third lose their house whilst in prison, two thirds lose their job, and about 40 per cent lose contact with their family. The Social Exclusion Unit report further warns that:

> There are also real dangers of mental and physical health deteriorating further, of life and thinking skills being eroded, and of prisoners being introduced to drugs. By aggravating the factors associated with reoffending, prison sentences can prove counter-productive as a contribution to crime reduction and public safety. (Social Exclusion Unit 2002)

Total institutions

Prisons are total institutions. Goffman defines them as: 'a place of residence and work where a large number of like-situated individuals, cut off from the wider society for an appreciable period of time, together lead an enclosed, formally administered round of life' (Goffman 1961: 11). Total institutions include secure mental health facilities whereas the US detention camp at Guantanamo Bay is another example of a total institution: cut off from the rest of the world, these places become worlds of their own with their own rules, realities and internal logic. The Stanford Prison Study conducted by Haney *et al*. (1973) (Key study below) highlights that. Once inside prison, an individual is stripped of most of his possessions, the roles they are accustomed to, their dignity, even their identity (Zimbardo 1973). In Goffman's words, 'he begins a series of abasements, degradations, humiliations' (Goffman 1961: 24).

Wandsworth Prison Landing Rules

HMP Wandsworth is committed to providing a safe and secure environment for prisoners and staff. Intimidation or violence is not tolerated. We aim to treat everyone with respect and to give an opportunity to use time spent here constructively.

Good behaviour is rewarded by the Incentives and Earned Privilege Scheme. Poor behaviour is challenged in the same scheme. If you follow the rules you may get more visits and greater access to private cash. For any serious breach of Prison Rules you may be placed on Governor's report.

The cell bell is for emergency use only. This is a serious matter. Staff respond to the bell as if your life is in danger. If you press the bell and it is not an emergency, you prevent the staff from responding to a real emergency.

You must be properly dressed at all times and be fully dressed between breakfast and tea. For health and safety reasons please refrain from wearing flip-flops on the landing. Outdoor jackets are to be worn outside only. Do not place a towel or any other material on or around your shoulders. You may be in bed with your shoes off but you must remain dressed during the day.

You must have the landing staff's permission to leave the landing. Staff are responsible for the safety of all prisoners on the landing. If you are not where you are supposed to be, a member of staff will look for you.

When returning to the landing, you must inform landing staff. When returning to the landing, tell the staff that you have returned. If staff have to look for you, all other activities on the landing may be suspended until you are found.

Do not enter a prisoner's cell without permission. No matter what the reason, you must not enter any cell other than your own without permission. If you do, you run the risk of being called a thief and placing yourself in danger.

If you hear a whistle or an alarm on your wing, go to your cell immediately. A whistle or an alarm signifies an incident or emergency is happening. Once the situation is over, staff will unlock you.

Keep your cell clean and tidy. You will have an opportunity to mop out your cell. In addition, each cell has a dustpan and brush and we encourage you to use it to sweep out your cell as needed.

Respect the rules on smoking. HMP Wandsworth is a non-smoking environment. Smoking is permitted only in your cell and on the exercise yard.

Never throw anything out of cell windows. Throwing things out of the windows (particularly food) creates hazards for everyone and only attracts rats and other vermin.

Never pass any substance out of the cell window to another cell. If you do this, it could be assumed that you are passing a prohibited substance.

Never shout out of the cell windows or on the landings. Again, we all live here. Shouting out of the windows or on the landings disturbs everyone.

Source: HMP Wandsworth Prison Induction Manual (2005)

Road traffic accident. Should reckless drivers be sent to prison?
Photo courtesy of Jan Brayley (Hampshire Constabulary).

Does prison work?

Before we can examine whether prison works, we need to decide what it means for prison to 'work'. If prison is simply about keeping offenders off the streets, then of course prison works, at least for the 80,000 inmates held at present. If the aim of imprisonment is to give offenders the punishment they deserve, then it is also easily argued that prison achieves that. Thus, for the purposes of *incarceration* (keeping offenders off the streets) and of *retribution* (giving them the punishment they deserve) you could say that prison works.

Key study: The Stanford Prison Experiment

Study of prisoners and guards in a simulated prison

Aim
To test the 'dispositional hypothesis' that the state of prison life is due to the nature of those who populate it. In other words, that prisons are tough places because those inside are dangerous people.

Method
Participants
Twenty-two participants were selected who had responded to a newspaper advertisement asking for male volunteers to participate in a psychological study of 'prison life'. They were to be paid $15 per day. Each participant was extensively screened and interviewed and only those judged to be the most stable, mature and least anti social were selected. They were mostly male, middle class and white. The participants were assigned to the role of either 'prisoner' or 'guard' completely randomly.

Procedure
A mock prison was built in the basement of Stanford University, lavatories were made into cells. In each cell was a mattress, sheet and pillow. The cells were small and unlit. The guards had their own quarters.

Prior to the study, the guards attended an orientation meeting. They were instructed to 'maintain the reasonable degree of order within the prison necessary for its effective functioning'. Haney *et al.* intentionally gave only minimal guidelines of what it meant to be a guard. Prior to the prisoners becoming incarcerated, the guards also assisted in completing the cell complex, for example by setting up their quarters, and furnishing the cells.

Participants in the prisoner role were unexpectedly 'arrested' at their homes, charged with a crime, advised of their legal rights, handcuffed, searched and transported to a police station. The prisoners were blindfolded and subsequently driven to the mock prison. Upon arrival they were stripped, deloused and made to stand alone naked in the cell yard. They were given their uniform, had their mugshot taken, put in a cell and ordered to remain silent.

The uniforms ascribed to prisoners consisted of a loose fitting smock with their identification number on the front and back, no underclothes, a chain and lock around one ankle, rubber sandals and a nylon stocking cap. The guards' uniform consisted of khaki shirts and trousers, a whistle, a police night stick and reflective sunglasses.

Results

Participants almost immediately internalised the prison environment. Prisoners adopted a passive response while the guards became dominant and quickly wielded their power. The guards' interactions with prisoners were hostile, negative, affrontive and dehumanising. Five prisoners experienced adverse reactions symptomatic of emotional depression, crying, rage and acute anxiety and had to be released early.

Haney et al. argue that all participants went beyond role playing and were not displaying *demand characteristics*. The guards exhibited what Haney et al. describe as 'pathology of power' and enjoyed their almost complete control over their prisoners. Afterwards, guards described this power as 'exhilarating'. Aggression and hostility intensified whenever there was any threat from the prisoners and that became the baseline from which any new hostility arose. The cruellest guards became role models for the other guards. Not to be tough was considered a sign of weakness and those guards who were not hostile never once challenged or contradicted the aggressive ones.

The prisoners developed 'pathological prisoners' syndrome'. Some prisoners became 'sick' whilst others were excessively obedient siding with the guards against a solitary fellow prisoner on hunger strike. Instead of supporting him, he was treated as a 'trouble maker' and received no support from his comrades. The prisoners also referred to each other by their ID numbers even in non-role related situations. Reality and individuality seemed to be suspended and the environment became increasingly hostile.

Discussion

We can reject the notion of the dispositional hypothesis in favour of a situational hypothesis. This means it is situations that cause the behaviour observed, not the other way around.

Source: Haney et al. (1973).

But when we talk about whether 'prison works', we often talk about *deterrence* and *rehabilitation*. Deterrence is the idea that the prison experience (or the threat of prison) deters individuals from committing crime. *Individual deterrence* refers to that effect for individual prisoners: once inside, they'll think twice about reoffending, or so the reasoning goes. *General deterrence* refers to its effect on others: when someone has been sent to prison, that makes other people stop and think about committing crime as well.

The other way in which prison can work is through *rehabilitation*. That involves 'improving' the offender. If offenders acquire skills that will help them get a job upon release, that will enhance their chances of desisting from crime. As many prisoners lack such basic skills, that is an obvious area of working with prisoners to enhance their prospects. In addition, offence specific issues might need addressing. Violent offenders might be taught new ways of solving conflicts. Sex offenders may benefit from interventions that can alter cognitive distortions. Thus, the reasoning behind rehabilitation in prison is that when they are inside, prisoners are equipped with skills and knowledge that will help them to find their feet back into society.

When you ask offenders in prison, many will say that prison has taught them a lesson and that the major reason for not offending again is the fact that they do not want to come back. Despite those good intentions, the reality is often different (Burnett and Maruna 2004).

Of those released from prison or who completed a form of community punishment in 2004, 57.6 per cent had reoffended within two years (Cunliffe and Shepherd 2007). Those released from prison did worse with 64 per cent reoffending. Those who undertook a community order reoffended in 50.5 per cent of cases. For community orders, the picture is mixed with certain orders seemingly more successful than others. Those on the receiving end of a Drug Treatment and Testing Order (DTTO) re-offended in over 80 per cent of cases. Recently, Drug Treatment and Testing orders have been replaced by Drug Referral Requirements (DRR), but the underlying principles remain the same.

Psychologist in profile

'Working with women prisoners is certainly not for everyone'

Karen Pinder
Senior Psychologist
HM Prison Send

'I completed my BSc in Psychology at University College, London. After graduating, I worked in research for several years, but I really wanted a more 'hands on' job. I applied to the Prison Service as a trainee forensic psychologist. I completed my MSc in Forensic and Legal Psychology at Leicester University through distance learning.

I have worked for the Prison Service for over twelve years. During the past four years I have worked as a psychologist and group therapist on the only therapeutic community (TC) for female prisoners in England and Wales, at HMP Send. The women here usually have long-standing psychological problems, often exacerbated by substance misuse. They attend group therapy (for groups of up to eight women) three times a week, and on the other two mornings the whole community meets to discuss community issues. Anything – and everything! – can come up at a community meeting. The aim of this is to encourage people to attempt to resolve situations they have found difficult rather than 'sitting on' their anger and then acting it out towards innocent bystanders.

Many women have committed serious acts of violence following years of abuse. They bottled up their anger until they became so overwhelmed that they were unable to control their behaviour. As you might imagine, this kind of work is quite exhausting as well as immensely satisfying. It's certainly not for everyone: as a therapist, you are exposed to some extremely upsetting and disturbing material. Sometimes you are on the receiving end of negative emotional outbursts. As we work with the women for a long time (they must commit to at least a year in therapy), we are able to see the changes they make, and when you witness someone taking control of their life you are reminded of why this work is so rewarding.

Unfortunately, if you work in prisons for long enough you will be exposed to suicide and self-harm. Working with individuals who self-harm or are suicidal is both challenging and upsetting. I don't necessarily think of myself as an expert in this matter, but I do think the contact I've had with people who either self-harm or attempt suicide has allowed me a deeper understanding of it. I think, or I hope, that this has helped me work more effectively in this field.'

The Home Office have formulated seven pathways in order to facilitate offender resettlement after prison. These are:

1 Accommodation;
2 Education, training and employment;
3 Mental and physical health;
4 Drugs and alcohol;
5 Finance, benefits and debt;
6 Children and families of offenders;
7 Attitudes, thinking and behaviour.

As pathway seven is the one that attracts more psychological research we shall investigate some of the programmes that relate to that.

Policies behind bars. Whether prison works depends on your view of its aims.
Photo courtesy of Francis Pakes.

Evaluate

When looking at the relative success of prison versus community punishment remember the following points:

- Reconviction rates are calculated using official statistics. Remember the drawbacks of that method (see Chapter 1).
- Individuals sent to prison are more likely to be 'hardened' criminals. They might be more likely to reoffend.
- The question is not only whether a punishment works but also whether they are appropriate.

Therefore, we cannot conclude from such data whether prison 'works' or not and the same is true for community punishments

Restorative justice

Restorative justice seems a novel approach to deal with offending behaviour, but in fact, it is probably many centuries old. Proponents of restorative justice argue that in regular courts, the victim is largely ignored and the offender passively sits in the dock with barristers doing the business for both prosecution and defence. That is not right, they argue. Most crimes are a wrong between an offender and a victim, and that is where the wrong should be put right.

The idea behind restorative justice is that there should be a connection made between victim and offender. That will make the offender realise the consequences of their actions, and will allow the victim to explain how they have been affected. It allows the offender to apologise, and to consider ways in which the damage can be repaired (Marshall 1999).

Restorative justice in its modern form originated in New Zealand, but Australia's model from Wagga Wagga has served as an example world wide. It involves a get together of all parties, a Family Group Conference. The idea is that the victim attends with family members or another source of support, the offender also with relatives, and other involved parties. A conference coordinator makes sure that the victim has ample opportunity to discuss the crime and its effects but so can the offender. The aim is to denounce the crime without necessarily denouncing the offender. They can apologise and an action plan is put in place that allows the offender to put right the damage.

Another function of such conferences is 'reintegrative shaming'. Where regular criminal justice can be stigmatising which can bring about its own negative effects, restorative justice is aimed at invoking a sense of regret and shame within the offender and their family, after which no stigmatising or exclusion needs to take place. In that way, restorative justice hopes to avoid the negative effects associated with regular criminal justice (Braithwaite 1989).

Restorative justice also occurs in the UK, in particular with minor offences where the offender does not deny their guilt. By taking part in such a conference they can avoid a criminal trial. The question, as with many criminal justice interventions is whether they are successful. When we take a procedural perspective on restorative justice, it can certainly seem to be successful. Where conferences take place, both victims and offenders tend to be positive about them. Most offenders apologise and most victims say that they see a benefit of having met the offender face to face (Miers *et al.* 2001). However, it must be said that in the UK, such face to face meetings do not occur very often. Most victims say that they prefer mediated contact, which often involves the offender writing a letter to the victim (Shapland *et al.* 2006). In addition, the evidence on whether restorative justice prevents further offending is mixed (Hayes 2005). That makes us wonder whether we should promote restorative justice because it is an ethical way of dealing with offenders, but perhaps not necessarily a highly effective instrument.

Working with offenders

Within the UK and many other countries such as Canada and the US, it is accepted that working with offenders requires a *cognitive-behavioural approach*. Cognition is about thinking. It involves recognising patterns of distorted thinking which allows the commission of offences. It also aims at increasing the understanding of the impact their crimes have on victims. The behavioural aspect of working with offenders involves achieving behavioural change. It is unlikely that cognitive change alone will produce lasting change and the same is true for behaviour modification alone. The two need to go hand in hand in order to achieve lasting results (Cann *et al.* 2005).

Cognitive-behavioural interventions usually involve working in groups. These are often between six and twelve offenders with one or two facilitators. The activities involve discussions, role play, solving dilemmas etcetera, and usually happen in a series of two hourly sessions. We will examine the programme *Reasoning and Rehabilitation* that focuses intensively on thinking patterns. Subsequently we shall look at the *Sex Offender Treatment Programme* (*SOTP*) that involves work on general offending issues but also specific work to do with sex offending.

Reasoning and rehabilitation

The programme *Reasoning and Rehabilitation* was developed in Canada. It aims to teach offenders to react more appropriately to situations that would trigger their offending behaviour. It teaches cognitive and behavioural skills, such as social skills, lateral thinking, critical thinking, values, assertiveness, and social perspective taking (i.e. placing yourself in someone else's shoes) (Ross *et al.* 1988). The programme is designed to teach offenders 'how to think, not what to think' (Robinson and Porporino 2001: 180). The programme involves 36 two-hour-sessions with groups of six to twelve participants, and often it involves several two hour sessions a week.

Does it work? Joy Tong and Farrington conducted a meta-analysis (Joy Tong and Farrington 2006). They found that on the whole, the programme reduces reoffending by 14 per cent. Therefore Joy Tong and Farrington conclude that 'the R&R programme seems to be an effective intervention programme' (Joy Tong and Farrington 2006: 19). Reasoning and Rehabilitation was equally successful for high-risk as it was for low-risk offenders. A further important finding is that those who fail to complete the programme actually perform worse than those who never took part in the first place. That makes it important that those who start should finish, and that only those offenders who are suitable are admitted.

There are criticisms against Reasoning and Rehabilitation. They mainly focus on the fact that offending is predominantly blamed on poor thinking. Other factors such as poverty, addiction and social exclusion are not part of the programme. In addition, the effectiveness of the programme is measured via recidivism rates. We have seen earlier that that is a very crude way of measuring offending behaviour. That said, what evaluations there are, are positive.

Activity

Is a reduction of 14 per cent as achieved by the Reasoning and Rehabilitation programme a positive result? Debate to what extent poor thinking is the main reason for crime. Also, remember that we might change an offender's thinking but we cannot change the situation they walk into after release from prison.

The Sex Offender Treatment Programme (SOTP)

The Sex Offender Treatment Programme (SOTP) began in 1991. It addresses both the offender's cognitions (distorted thinking patterns that facilitate offending), and their behaviour. The latter involves reducing sexual arousal to inappropriate fantasies.

The SOTP consists of several components. The core programme aims to increase the offender's motivation to avoid reoffending and to develop the self-management skills necessary to achieve this (Beech *et al.* 1998). Offenders' motivation is increased by working on cognitive distortions and increasing empathy for their victims. Self-management skills relate to *relapse prevention*. That involves learning to recognise early signs of wanting to reoffend (certain fantasies for instance) and learning to recognise situations in which offending behaviour might occur. The techniques deployed include group discussion and brainstorming, role-play exercises, and use of videos and written materials provided by victims.

The SOTP will only be successful if certain areas are successfully addressed. The first is *denial and minimisation* (these are sometimes called neutralisation techniques (see box). Sex offenders often deny both the full extent of their sexually deviant behaviour and the risk they pose of reoffending. Breaking down denial is important. The second is *damage to victims*. Sex offenders frequently demonstrate little remorse and do not appear to recognise the damage they do to their victims. Victim empathy needs to be improved. The third is *deviant sexual fantasies*. Treatment is aimed at teaching the offender to control deviant arousal and to develop arousal to non-deviant fantasies instead. The next key feature of the SOTP programme is *relapse prevention*. Based on the work of Marlatt and Gordon (1985) in the field of addictions, the treatment aim is to get offenders to recognise situations, feelings, moods and types of thought which put them at risk of reoffending. The next is *lifestyle and personality*. Problems with expressing themselves assertively, low self-esteem, and the failure to develop a capacity for intimacy in adult relationships appear to be common characteristics of sex offenders (Marshall 1989). That requires in-depth skill building. The final part of the programme is *sex education*. Many offenders have poor knowledge about sex and the emotional component of sexual relations. Education in that area will increase the likelihood that offenders upon release will be able to engage in appropriate intimate and sexual relationships.

Neutralisation techniques

Sykes and Matza (1957) described a number of so-called neutralisation techniques. They are utilised by offenders to minimise their sense of culpability, or as ways in which their offending behaviour is justified. They include 'denial of responsibility', suggesting that it was not their fault anyway; 'denial of victim' suggesting that the victim 'was asking for it', or 'denial of harm', for instance by saying that burglary victims have insurance anyway.

But is it effective? Many people hold strong views on sex offenders. They are often regarded as highly devious and untreatable: they simply will not change. But is that true? Can a programme of about 86 two-hour-sessions change an offender such that they are significantly less likely to reoffend? Beech *et al.* (1998) carried out an extensive evaluation on the effectiveness of SOTP with sex offenders.

They followed 82 child sex abusers and established their levels of denial, pro-offending attitudes, predisposing personality factors (such as low self-esteem and failure to accept responsibility for their actions), and relapse prevention skills. Significant improvements were found in all areas. The programme was most effective for men with low deviancy and low levels of denial (as you perhaps might expect): 59 per cent showed an overall improvement, and 84 per cent showed a reduction in pro-offending attitudes. The results for high deviancy men were not so positive, with only 14–17 per cent of men showing overall improvement. Fifty-six men agreed to be interviewed nine months later. It was found that those who showed a reduction in pro-offending attitudes had maintained their relapse prevention skills. Those whose attitudes had not changed quickly lost those skills.

Prison wing. Is prison a suitable place for rehabilitation?
Photo courtesy of Francis Pakes.

Ireland (2004) evaluated an anger management programme in prison. In total 50 prisoners took twelve one-hour-sessions run over a three-day period. Their mean age was 19 years. They took part in groups of about ten, with two facilitators. The programme involved a number of activities such as group discussions, role play, watching videos and various exercises. It addressed issues of anger and aggression, triggers to anger and the importance of behaviour, thoughts and feelings. Afterwards they were assessed using the Wing Behaviour Checklist and an Anger Management Assessment. Most prisoners who took the course improved on one or both of these measures and better than a control group (a group of young prisoners that were deemed suitable for the course but had not taken it). It demonstrates that prison programmes can work, at least in the short term whilst the offender is still detained. It did not assess whether the good outcomes would persist after release.

What to do with an offender who is seriously mentally unwell?

Decisions in relation to crime, mental health, and dangerousness
Based on a true account

Tom is an educated and intelligent man. He was an only child with a disturbed and chaotic upbringing. He never knew his father. Tom has highly rigid beliefs about women, sexuality and the Christian faith. One day he became psychotic and delusional: he believed that his friend was the devil. In a distressed state, he was found by local police officers who agreed to transport him to hospital. En route he subjected the escorting female police officer to a serious sexual assault, leaving her severely traumatised. As Tom was consequently detained in hospital under the *Mental Health Act 1983* The Crown Prosecution Service deemed therefore that it was not in the public interest to pursue the case and consequently Tom was never charged nor convicted.

In hospital Tom took regular medication, stabilised and was soon free of psychotic symptoms. Although still quite fragile, he was able to work and pursue leisure activities. He attended a local book club where he befriended an elderly lady. One evening by mutual consent he stayed over in the guest bedroom.

Overnight a dramatic change had taken place in Tom. He entered the lady's bedroom, and subjected her to a serious sexual assault and held her captive for six hours. Throughout, Tom was obsessed with religious ideas, prayed out loud as he subjected her to a harrowing ordeal.

Tom was charged with false imprisonment and sexual assault. He was detained in a hospital, rather than a remand prison, under the *Mental Health Act 1983*, where he took regular medication and, reluctantly, engaged in therapy. It was identified that he had deficiencies in dealing with others and showed no remorse over his crime. He felt that the 'mental illness' was responsible for the crime rather than he himself. He also expressed no empathy towards his victim. He was very self-centred and highly rigid in his attitudes.

In court Tom was found not guilty by reason of insanity and directed to return to hospital for an indefinite period of time under the *Mental Health Act 1983*.

Patients convicted of an offence but given a hospital order as opposed to a prison sentence have the right to apply to a Mental Health Review Tribunal and seek their discharge. Such Tribunals must balance the rights of the patient, with public protection and take into account the feelings of victims. Tom made such an application.

However, the tribunal acknowledged the following risk factors:

- Tom has limited capacity to empathise;
- He perceives himself as a victim;
- He dissociates himself from his crimes;
- He blames other people for his problems;
- He tends to deny and to minimise the hurt he has caused;
- He has distorted views of women and sexuality.

There were also concerns that Tom's mental illness could reappear should he not comply with medication and treatment. Also because of his intelligence and the fact that he presents well there is a fear that Tom could actively seek out new victims. After all, although never convicted, there is evidence of two serious sexual assaults in a year. However, mindful of the risk factors including the risk of reoffending and relapse of his mental state, the Tribunal concluded that on the day of the hearing that Tom's mental illness was under good control and that he did not fulfil the criteria for continued detention in hospital. Consequently, Tom was granted his discharge from hospital with follow-up from community psychiatric services.

In order to enhance victim empathy and to help realise what he has done, Tom met with his victim. As a devout Christian, she was able to forgive him, and move on. The meeting helped her healing process but Tom remained unaffected, seemingly unconcerned about her feelings.

The performance of such programmes in prison must always be evaluated against the prison backdrop. Prisons can be harsh environments in which preparing for release is not always easy. In addition, the bulk of such programmes take place in a group setting. No doubt some groups are more cohesive and supportive than others. Thus, even though the results achieved by such programmes are positive, they are also no more than moderate at the same time. However, when we remember the extent of poor literacy, and the high frequency of mental illness, suicide attempts and self harm in prison we should perhaps be pleasantly surprised that they work as well as they do.

Community orders

Community orders can be imposed by a judge when it is felt that prison is unsuitable because it is either too harsh or because the aims of a specific penalty can also be achieved outside prison. It has been found that many programmes that might run both in prison and in the community yield better results outside of prison. We can think of two reasons why that is so. Firstly, we might not be comparing like with like, with more serious offenders being placed in prison. Thus, allocation into experimental groups is not random. Such research designs are at best *quasi experimental*. Secondly, the nature of prison life can conspire against offenders successfully tackling their own deficits. With that in mind, we will examine community punishment in case of two groups of offenders that offer specific challenges. These are sex offenders in the community and prolific offenders who receive a community order to tackle their drug habit.

Sex offenders in the community

Mandeville-Norden and Beech (2004) report that there are three programmes to which sex offenders who are managed in the community can be subjected to. They are all versions of the Sex Offender Groupwork Programme (SOGP). One of these, the West Midlands version of SOGP consists of three parts, an induction module which lasts for 50 hours; more serious or high risk offenders then take the Long Term Therapy programme, which runs for a total of 190 hours. The third component, of the SOGP is about Relapse Prevention and lasts 50 hours.

For most offenders, the court has sentenced them to attend such programmes. Attendance therefore is compulsory. The programmes are taught in groups. It was found that both group cohesion and the leadership style of programme tutors were important factors in the success of such programmes (Beech and Fordham 1997).

Drug treatment

A judge can impose a Drug Treatment and Testing Order (DTTO) on a defendant. It is aimed at those offenders who have committed multiple crimes to finance their drug misuse. The length of the order can be from six months to three years. The DTTO has three main requirements:

- A treatment requirement – to undergo 'treatment' at a specified place (residential centre or as an out-patient while continuing to reside in the community) for a set period of between six months and three years;
- A testing requirement – an offender who is subject to DTTO must be tested regularly for drug use and the results, together with the treatment provider's reports, provide a clear indication of progress;
- A court review requirement – the courts have a formal and vital role in the 'reviewing' process. These reviews are designed both to motivate the offender and give the court confidence that the treatment is being complied with.

Does it work? At first sight, the reconviction data do not look promising: no less than 80 per cent reoffend within two years. DTTOs are among the penalties that most often precede reoffending. In addition, it was found that completion of the order is important: of those who received a DTTO but failed to complete it, 91 per cent reoffended. Completion rates were in the order of 30 per cent, and an increase in the number of people completing DTTOs is likely to increase its success.

Powell and Bamber (2007) interviewed 107 offenders on a DTTO and found that they were positive about the way they were treated and felt that the order provided positive incentives to overcome their addiction. Unfortunately, the programme did not involve a measure on reoffending. Naeem *et al.* (2007) carried out a controlled trial comparing individuals on a DTTO against similar individuals who received 'standard care'. After twelve months both groups were compared on a range of variables such as addiction, drug use and a measure of general health. They did find that DTTOs were more effective in reducing drug use than 'treatment as usual'.

Psychologist in profile

'When you work with long term prisoners, you need to have belief in what you do'

Charlie Hodges
Chartered Forensic Psychologist
HM Prison Parkhurst, Isle of Wight

'I actually started to study sociology at Reading University. It was combined with psychology, which I really enjoyed. I therefore decided to make psychology the basis of my career. My first proper job was as a Psychology Assistant, and then I acquired a trainee post in the prison service on the Isle of Wight. I have been involved with the delivery of offender programmes in prison. In 2004 I finished my MSc degree at the University of Portsmouth.

I have delivered a range of offender programmes. That includes Reasoning and Rehabilitation, which offenders often take early in their sentence. A more advanced programme is CSCP, a Cognitive Self Change Programme. It is an 18-month programme for violent high-risk offenders. Some of these are on a life sentence and have committed very serious offences. In a programme that takes 18 months, you cannot stay on the surface. If you do not engage with it, or you're simply pretending to, this will become obvious. The motivation of individuals to take part is most important. It is essential that interventions are targeted at prisoners who will benefit.

For every prisoner who attends a group a range of treatment needs are identified and from there we recommend programmes to address those. It is often focused on insight, on getting the offender to understand their own risky patterns of thinking. Those thinking patterns need to change. I have worked with offenders whose first instinct is to solve any problem with violence. They need to get that out of their heads and they need the skills to approach situations in a different manner. I have seen profound change in some of the people I have worked with.

Another part of my work involves Risk Assessment Reports for life sentence prisoners who might be up for release, or for a change in prison regime. We prepare their risk factors as part of a multi-disciplinary team in the early stages of their sentences. Apart from psychologists these boards consist of prison officers and probation officers. Reports are then written which focus on how much insight they have gained into their offending. These then go to the Parole Board. The Parole Board is an independent body that makes risk assessments about prisoners to decide who may safely be released into the community and who must remain inside.

In order to write such a report we look at all the information, the way the offence was committed and specific risk factors, such as violence, drugs, and poor emotional management. We try to evaluate the level of insight that an offender has into their risks, their willingness to work on these risks and the progress made. It is all about reducing the risk of reoffending, and we use all the information and skills we have to contribute to that.

In order to work with long term prisoners, you need a belief and passion for what you do. You do see change in individuals, but on the other hand, you also encounter people who left prison only to come back after further offences. That can be demoralising – but you have to remind yourself that in many cases you do make a difference.'

Enforcing community orders

Community orders are often enforced with the application of electronic monitoring, or *electronic tagging*. That involves a piece of technology that is usually fixed around one ankle of the individual and that allows for the establishment of the whereabouts of that individual at any point in time. It is particularly relevant for offenders who are out in the community but upon whom certain restrictions have been placed. Such restrictions can include not to come near schools, a shopping centre or near the house of a victim.

A further means of controlling sex offenders is via the Sex Offender Registration database. Persons convicted of a sex offence are required to register themselves with the local police. It must be done by the offender within three days of conviction or release from prison. The data feed into a national database called ViSOR. For minor offences, the registration is temporary, for five, seven or ten years. Serious offenders stay on the register for life. A change of address must be passed on to the police within 14 days, and whenever an offender is away for 14 days, that must be notified as well. Not complying with the requirement is an arrestable offence. It carries a prison sentence of up to five years. ViSOR is a valuable source of information and helps keeping tabs on registered violent and sexual offenders in local areas.

There is no general access to the database. Local residents cannot check whether there are registered sex offenders in their area. Although newspaper the *News of the World* campaigned for the 'naming and shaming' of child sex offenders in particular, such community notification does not exist and is unlikely to occur in the near future. The main reason is the fear that that will spark riots, violence and vigilantism, which would hurt innocent people. In addition, it might force those on the register into hiding where they might do even more harm. Then Home Secretary David Blunkett (2002) noted: 'We cannot open the register to vigilantes who do not understand the difference between paediatricians and paedophiles.'

Chemical castration?

Surgical castration is an irreversible operation that involves removing the testes. In the first half of the twentieth century this method was used in several European countries, but it has long since been abandoned as a treatment for sex offenders. In the US, however, the use of so-called *chemical castration* is quite widespread. Chemical castration is a hormonal treatment. It involves the injection of drugs to reduce a man's testosterone levels. There are two drugs that tend to be used. In the US it is MPA (or Depo-Provera) and in Canada and several European countries CPA is used. They work via weekly injections.

The offender will usually feel a reduction in sexual drive, a decrease in sexual fantasies and may become impotent. That will reduce the chance of reoffending in two ways. The first is that the offender might be more likely to control these much reduced sexual urges. The second is that that might 'free up' the offender's mind and focus it on other things. As one US offender explained: 'I realised I could walk down the street, see boys I found sexually attractive, and not be possessed by thoughts about having sex with them ... It took that edge off' (Russell 1997: 431).

Testosterone

Hormones are chemical messengers that help regulate the body. Male sex hormones are called *androgens*. The main female hormones are *oestrogen* and *progesterone*, but both occur in both men and women, but at very different rates. In males testosterone is mainly produced by the testes. Apart from regulating libido it is also involved with muscular development.

The US state of California was the first to introduce chemical castration in 1997. It can be applied to high-risk repeat sex offenders with a victim of younger than 13 years old. Chemical castration can be a condition of release from prison, for a set period of time (the licence period). It is not carried out in conjunction with any cognitive-behavioural treatment alongside it (Connelly and Williamson 2000; Carpenter 2007).

Activity

Chemical castration of sex offenders: are you in favour?

Chemical castration offers benefits: it reduces reoffending (but mostly so when in combination with other interventions); it might allow some offenders out of prison because their risk of offending is much reduced; and it is reversible.

On the other hand, we must ensure that offenders comply with medication; there are medical side effects that can be quite serious; and it seems to suggest that sex offending is primarily caused by hormones, as chemical castration suppresses the production of testosterone.

What do you think the main causes of sex offending are? Refer back to the approaches to criminal psychology (Chapter 1).

From the research evidence it seems that chemical castration is more effective than most other counselling or treatment options (Lösel and Schmucker 2005). But there are methodological difficulties with the studies that report it (see box). Carpenter (2007) argues that if chemical castration were to be introduced in the UK, it should be for serious repeat offenders only and in conjunction with cognitive-behavioural interventions that, as we have seen, are moderately successful for many sex offenders by themselves.

What punishment works best?

Why the perfect study does not exist

Studies that assess the effectiveness of a certain form of punishment usually follow a group of offenders who received that punishment and after a period of time establish whether they reoffended. Such designs have several shortcomings. The problems are to do with the following areas.

How to measure reoffending?

Reoffending is often established via official statistics. In Chapter 1 we discovered that most crime does not feature in those statistics. Reoffending rates will therefore be lower than the true offending rates of the individuals in the study.

In addition, reoffending is usually established over a certain period of time. That is often in the order of two years. It is known, however, that for some offenders the risk of reoffending goes down over time, whereas others remain high risk for many more years (Prentky *et al.* 1997). If you take a two-year window, you will not be able to tell the difference between those groups. But taking a longer period of time means that we will not know the outcome of a certain punishment for many years to come.

Measuring outcomes via other means

Because of the difficulties with measuring recidivism, researchers sometimes use so-called *proxy* measures, variables that are easier to measure and should still be informative. They can for instance assess an offender's behaviour during sessions or ask them whether they thought the programme was helpful. You might question whether that is the best way of establishing whether a punishment 'works'.

The nature of the control group

The best studies measure reoffending and compare that with a control group. But control groups are difficult to put together. Should we compare prison with community sentences we are not comparing the same type of offender: the more dangerous and prolific offenders will go to prison and not take community punishment. It is a problem with using a *quasi-experimental design*. That is an experimental design in which two or more groups receive a different treatment and the effect of that treatment is established, but there is no random assignment to groups: the researcher has no full control over the independent variable (type of punishment): the sentence given is for the judge to decide, not the researcher.

Lack of experimental control

In the real world of crime and punishment many factors are beyond an experimenter's control. Researchers often cannot control the group dynamics in group sessions or the context in which certain interventions are carried out. Researchers may not know about hidden variables such as mental health issues, or drugs problems. In addition, it is possible that unsuitable offenders enter certain programmes. They might be destined to fail and make the programme look bad as a result.

Such shortcomings cannot easily be remedied. The perfect study in a real life setting is simply not feasible.

Conclusion

Most people have an opinion on how we deal with offenders. Punishment is often seen to be too lenient or otherwise inappropriate. But we must remember that punishment suffers from a fundamental problem: it is imposed with several aims in mind and those aims often do not go together. Prison is a place of suffering. If punishment is about suffering then prison is the right place for it. But prisons are also about rehabilitation. Suffering and rehabilitation do not go hand in hand. That is a problem we cannot solve: prisons probably should be bleak and austere places. They probably should deter. But on the other hand, prisons must be places of opportunity. Offenders who enter prison addicted and illiterate, should come out healthy and skilled. But it is difficult for prisons to be all things to all people.

What is true for prisons is true for other forms of punishment as well. They are instruments of controversy and contradiction. That adds another layer of complexity to the question of whether they work or not. It makes the area of criminal psychology extra difficult in terms of research methodology. But is also makes it important and exciting: the outcomes can affect the lives of many offenders and victims alike.

References

Aguirre, A. and Baker, D.V. (1993) Racial prejudice and the death penalty: a research note. *Social Issues*, 20, 150–6.

Ainsworth, P. (2001) *Offender Profiling and Crime Analysis*. Cullompton: Willan.

Aleixo P.A. and Norris C.E. (2000) Personality and moral reasoning in young offenders. *Personality and Individual Differences*, 28, 609–623.

Alison, L., Goodwill, A. and Alison, E. (2005) Guidelines for profilers. In L. Alison (ed.). *The Forensic Psychologist's Casebook*. Cullompton: Willan, pp. 235–77.

Alison, L., Smith, M.D., and Morgan,K. (2003a) Interpreting the accuracy of offender profiles. *Psychology, Crime and Law*, 9, 185–95.

Alison, L., Smith, M.D., Eastman, O., and Rainbow, L. (2003b) Toulmin's philosophy of argument and its relevance to offender profiling. *Psychology, Crime and Law*, 9, 173–83.

Amnesty International (1999) *Killing with prejudice*. Available online: www.amnesty.org/en/report/info/AMR51/052/1999.

Anderson, C.A. (2001) Heat and violence. *Current Directions in Psychological Science*, 10, 33–8.

Anderson, C.A., Anderson, K.B., Dorr, N., DeNeve, K.M., and Flanagan, M. (2000) Temperature and aggression. *Advances in Experimental Social Psychology*, 32, 63–133.

Anderson, R.C., and Pichert, J.S. (1978) Recall of previously unrecallable information following in shift in perspective. *Journal of Verbal Learning and Verbal Behaviour*, 17, 1–12.

Asch, S. (1956) Studies of independence and conformity: A minority of one against a unanimous majority. *Psychological Monographs*, 70, 416 (whole issue).

Ashkar, P.J., & Kenny, D.T. (2007) Nonsexual offenders' moral reasoning of adolescent male offenders: Comparison of sexual and nonsexual offenders. *Criminal Justice and Behavior*, 34, 108–18.

Baldus, D.C., Pulaski, C., and Woodworth, G. (1983) Comparative review of death sentences: An empirical study of the Georgia experience. *Journal of Criminal Law and Criminology*, 74, 661–753.

Baldus, D.C., Woodworth, G. and Pulaski, C. (1990) *Equal Justice and the Death Penalty: A Legal and Empirical Analysis.* Boston: Northeastern University Press.

Baldwin, J. (1993) Police interview techniques: Establishing truth or proof? *British Journal of Criminology,* 33, 325–52.

Bandura, A., Ross, D., and Ross, S.A. (1961) Transmission of aggression through imitation of aggressive models. *Journal of Abnormal and Social Psychology,* 66, 3–11.

Barker, R., Dembo, T. and Lewin, K. (1941) Frustration and Aggression: An experiment with young children, *University of Iowa Studies in Child Welfare,* 18, 1–314.

Bartlett, F.C. (1932) *Remembering.* Cambridge: Cambridge University Press.

Bayley, D.H. (1994) *Police for the future.* New York: Oxford University Press.

BBC News (2005) *Rape convictions hit record low.* Available online: http://news.bbc.co.uk/1/hi/uk/4296433.stm, 25 February 2005.

Beech, A., Fisher, D. and Beckett, R. (1998) *Step 3: An evaluation of the Prison Sex Offender Treatment Programme.* London: Home Office, November 1998.

Beech, A. and Fordham, A.S. (1997) Therapeutic climate of sexual offender treatment programs. *Sexual Abuse: A Journal of Research and Treatment, 9,* 219–37.

Bensley, L. and Van Eenwyk, J. (2001) Video games and real life aggression: Review of the literature. *Journal of Adolescent Health,* 29, 144–57.

Berkowitz, L. (1993) *Aggression: Its Causes, Consequences and Control.* New York: McGraw-Hill.

Berkowitz, L. and Geen, R.G. (1966) Film violence and the cue propensities of available targets. *Journal of Personality and Social Psychology,* 3, 525–30.

Berkowitz, L. and Lepage (1967) Weapons as aggression-eliciting stimuli. *Journal of Personality and Social Psychology,* 7, 202–207.

Bindel, J. (2007) Crime and Punishment. The *Guardian, 20 April 2007.*

Binder, R.L. and McNiel, D.E. (1994) Staff gender and risk of assaults on doctors and nurses. *Bulletin of the American Academy for Psychiatry and Law,* 22, 545–50.

Blackburn, R. (1993) *The Psychology of Criminal Conduct.* Chichester: Wiley.

Blunkett, D. (2002) *Fighting Crime and Disorder at the Core of Social Justice.* Speech, 2 October 2002.

Bosely, S. (2007) Britain in Grip of Hidden Abuse Epidemic, says BMA. The *Guardian,* 20 June 2007.

Boudreaux, M., Lord, W. and Dutra, R. (1999) Child abduction: Age-based analyses of offender, victim and offense characteristics of 550 cases of alleged child disappearance. *Journal of Forensic Sciences,* 44, 539–53.

Braithwaite, J. (1989) *Crime, Shame and Reintegration.* Cambridge: Cambridge University Press.

Brewster, M.P. (2003) Power and control dynamics in prestalking and stalking situations. *Journal of Family Violence*, 18(4), 207–17.

British Crime Survey (2001) *The 2001 British Crime Survey: First results, England and Wales*. London: Home Office.

Brunner, H.G., Nelen, M., Breakefield, X.O., Ropers, H.H., and Van Oost, B.A. (1993) Abnormal behavior associated with a point mutation in the structural gene for Monoamine Oxidase A. *Science*, 262, 470–80.

Bryant, J. and Zillman, D. (1979) Effect of Intensification of Annoyance Through Unrelated Residual Excitation on Substantially Delayed Hostile Behavior. *Journal of Experimental Social Psychology*, 15, 470–80.

Budd, T. (1999) *Violence and Work: Findings from the British Crime Survey*. London: Home Office.

Budd, T. and Mattinson, J. with Myhill A. (2000) *The Extent and Nature of Stalking: Findings from the 1998 British Crime Survey*. Home Office Research Study 210. London: Home Office.

Bull, R. and McAlpine, S. (1998) Facial appearance and criminality. In: Memon, A., Vrij, A. and Bull, R. (eds) *Psychology and Law: Truthfulness, Accuracy and Credibility*. Maidenhead: McGraw Hill, 59–76.

Bullock, H.A. (1961) Significance of the racial factor in the length of prison sentences. *Journal of Criminal Law, Criminology and Police Science*, 52, 411–17.

Burnett, R. and Maruna, S. (2004) So 'Prison Works', Does It? The Criminal Careers of 130 Men Released from Prison under Home Secretary, Michael Howard. *Howard Journal of Criminal Justice*, 43, 390–404.

Cann, J., Falshaw, L, and Friendship, C. (2005) Understanding 'What Works': Accredited Cognitive Skills Programmes for young offenders. *Youth Justice*, 5, 165–79.

Canter, D. (1994) *Criminal Shadows: Inside the Mind of the Serial Killer*. London: Harper Collins.

Canter, D. and Kirby, S. (1995) Prior convictions of child molesters. *Science and Justice*, 35, 73–8.

Canter, D. and Larkin, P. (1993) The environmental range of serial rapists. *Journal of Environmental Psychology*, 13, 63–9.

Carpenter, K. (2007) The high-risk sex offender strategy in England and Wales: Is chemical castration an option? *Howard Journal of Criminal Justice*, 46, 16–31.

Cheit, R.E. (2005) *The archive: 101 corroborated cases of recovered memory*. Available online: tinyurl.com/42yj7

Christiansen, K.O. (1977) A review of studies of criminality among twins. In S.A. Mednick and K.O. Christiansen (eds.). *Biological Bases of Criminal Behavior*. New York: Gardiner Press.

Claridge, G. and Davis, C. (2003) *Personality and Psychological Disorders*. London: Arnold.

Clifford, B.R. and Richards, G. (1977) Comparison of recall by policemen and civilians under conditions of long and short durations of exposure. *Perceptual and Motor Skills*, 45, 39–45.

Colby, A., Kohlberg, L., Gibbs, J. And Lieberman, M. (1983) A longitudinal study of moral development. *Monographs of the Society for Research in Child Development,* 48, 1-2 (serial number 200).

Coleman, K., Jansson, K., Kaiza, P. and Reed, E. (2007) *Homicides, Firearm Offences and Intimate Violence 2005/2006.* Home Office Statistical Bulletin, 02/07.

Connelly, C. and Williamson, S. (2000) *A Review of the Research Literature on Serious Violent and Sexual Offenders.* Edinburgh: The Scottish Executive Central Research Unit.

Conti, R.P. (1999) The psychology of false confessions. *The Journal of Credibility Assessment and Witness Psychology,* 2, 14–36.

Cope, N. (2005) The range of issues in crime analysis. In: L. Alison (ed.) *The Forensic Psychologist's Casebook: Psychological Profiling and Criminal Investigation.* Cullompton: Willan, 90–113.

Copson, G. (1995) *Coals to Newcastle? A study of Offender Profiling, Part 1.* London: Home Office, Police Research Group.

Cowie, H., Jennifer, D. and Sharp, S. (2002) *Tackling Violence in Schools: A Report from the UK.* European Union: Connect initiative.

Crick, N.R. and Dodge, K.A. (1994) A review and reformulation of social information-processing mechanisms in children's social adjustment. *Psychological Bulletin,* 115, 74–101.

Crowther, C. (2007) *An Introduction to Criminology and Criminal Justice.* Basingstoke: Palgrave/MacMillan.

Cunliffe, J. and Shepherd, A. (2007) *Re-offending of Adults: Results from the 2004 Cohort.* Home Office Statistical Bulletin 06/07: London: Home Office RDS/NOMS.

Davies, A. (1997) Specific profile analysis: A data-based approach to offender profiling. In: J.L. Jackson and D. Bekerian (eds.) *Offender Profiling, Theory, Research and Practice.* Chichester: Wiley, 191–208.

Davies, G. (1999) The impact of television on the presentation and Reception of Children's Testimony. *International Journal of Law and Psychiatry,* 22, 214–56.

Death Penalty Information Center (2008) *Facts About the Death Penalty.* Available online: www.deathpenaltyinfo.org/FactSheet.pdf.

Deffenbacher, K.A. (1980) Eyewitness accuracy and confidence: Can we infer anything about their relationship? *Law and Human Behaviour,* 4, 243–60.

DePaulo, B.M., and Kashy, D.A. (1998) Everyday lies in close and casual relationships. *Journal of Personality and Social Psychology,* 70, 703–16.

DePaulo, B.M. and Morris, W.L. (2004) Discerning lies from truths: Behavioural cues to deception and the indirect pathway of intuition. In P.A. Granhag and Stromwall (eds). *The Detection of Deception in Forensic Contexts,* pp. 15–40. Cambridge: Cambridge University Press.

DePaulo, B.M., Kashy, D.A., Kirkendol, S.E., Wyer, M.M. and Epstein, J.A. (1996) Lying in everyday life. *Journal of Personality and Social Psychology,* 70, 979–95.

DePaulo, B.M., Lindsay, J.J., Malone, B.E., Muhlenbruck, L., Charton, K. and Cooper, H. (2003) Cues to description. *Psychological Bulletin*, 129, 74–118.

Diener, E., Fraser, S.C., Beaman, A.L. and Kelem, R.T (1976) Effects of deindividuation variables on stealing on Halloween trick-or-treaters. *Journal of Personality and Social Psychology*, 33, 178–83.

Dollard, J., Doob, L.W., Mowrer, O.H. and Sears, R.R. (1939) *Frustration and Aggression*. New Haven, CT, US: Yale University Press.

Douglas, J. and Ohlshaker, M. (1997) *Mindhunter: Inside the FBI Elite Serial Crime Unit*. London: Arrow.

Dwyer, (2001) *Angles on Criminal Psychology*. Cheltenham: Nelson Thornes.

Eberhardt, J.L, Davies, P.G., Purdie-Vaughns, V.J. and Johnson, S.L. (2006) Looking deathworthy: Perceived stereotypicality of black defendants predicts capital-sentencing outcomes. *Psychological Science*, 17, 383–86.

Efran, M. (1974) The effect of physical appearance on the judgement of guilt, interpersonal attraction and severity of recommended punishment in a simulated jury task. *Journal of Research on Personality*, 8, 45–54.

Ekman, P. (2003) Darwin, deception, and facial expression. *Annals of the New York Academy of Sciences*, 1000, 205–21.

Eysenck, H.J. (1964) *Crime and Personality*. London: Routledge and Kegan.

Eysenck, H.J. (1977) *Crime and Personality*. London: Granada.

Eysenck, H.J. and Eysenck, S.B.G. (1975) *The Eysenck Personality Questionnaire* London: Hodder and Stoughton.

Eysenck, H.J., Eysenck, S.B.G. and Barrett, P. (1985) *The Eysenck Personality Questionnaire (revised)* London: Hodder and Stoughton.

Eysenck, H.J. and Gudjonsson, G.H. (1989) *The Causes and Cures of Criminality*. New York: Plenum Press.

Eysenck, M. (2000) *Cognitive Psychology: A student's handbook*. Hove: Psychology Press.

Farrington, D.P. (1995) The development of offending and antisocial behaviour from childhood: key funding from the Cambridge study in delinquent development. *Journal of Child Psychology and Psychiatry*, 36, 929–64.

Farrington, D.P., Gill, M., Sam J., Waples, S.J. and Argomaniz, J. (2007) The effects of closed-circuit television on crime: Meta-analysis of an English national quasi-experimental multi-site evaluation. *Journal of Experimental Criminology*, 3, 21–38.

Ferraro, K. (1995) *Fear of Crime*. Albany, NY, US: University of New York Press.

Fisher, R.P. and Geiselman, R.E. (1992) *Memory-Enhancing Techniques for Investigative Interviewing: The Cognitive Interview*. Springfield: Charles C. Thomas.

Fisher, R.P., Geiselman, R.E. and Amador, M. (1989) Field test of the cognitive interview: Enhancing the recollection of actual victims and witnesses of crime. *Journal of Applied Psychology*, 74, 722–7.

Fisher, R.P., Geiselman, R.E. and Raymond, D.S. (1987) Critical analysis of police interviewing techniques. *Journal of Police Science and Administration,* 15, 177–85.

Fisher, R.P. and Reardon, M.C. (2007) Eyewitness identification. In: Carson, D., Milne, R., Pakes, F., Shalev, K. and Shawyer, A. (eds) *Applying Psychology to Criminal Justice.* Chichester: Wiley, 21–38.

Fitzgerald, M. (1994) *Ethnic Minorities and the Criminal Justice System.* Research bulletin, no. 35, 49–50.

Freud, S. (1923) *The Ego and the Id.* Harmondsworth: Penguin.

Freud, S. (1930) *Civilisation and its Discontents.* London: W.W. Norton.

Friedman, M. and Rosenman, R.H. (1974) *Type A Behaviour and your Heart.* New York: Harper Row.

Fritzon, K. (2005) Assessing the reliability of interviews with vulnerable witnesses. In: L. Alison (ed.) *The Forensic Psychologist's Casebook: Psychological Profiling and Criminal Investigation.* Cullompton: Willan, 278–96.

Geiselman, R.E. and Callot, R. (1990) Reverse versus forward order recall of script-based texts. *Applied Cognitive Psychology,* 4, 141–4.

Geiselman, R.E., Fisher, R.P., MacKinnon, D.P. and Holland, H.L. (1986) Enhancement of eyewitness memory with the cognitive interview. *American Journal of Psychology,* 99, 385–401.

Gibbs, J.C. (2003) *Moral Development and Reality: Beyond the Theories of Kohlberg and Hoffman.* London: Sage.

Gibbs, J.C. and Widaman, K.F. (1982) *Social Intelligence: Measuring the Development of Sociomoral Reflection.* Englewood Cliffs, NJ: Prentice-Hall.

Gleitman, H. (2003) *Psychology (6th edition).* New York: Norton.

Goffman, E. (1961) *Asylums: Essays on the Social Situation of Mental Patients and Other Inmates.* Harmondsworth: Penguin.

Gottfredson, M. and Hirschi, T. (1990) *A General Theory of Crime.* Stanford: Stanford University Press.

Granhag, P.A. and Vrij, A. (2005) Detecting deception. In N. Brewer and K.D. Williams (eds) *Psychology and Law: An Empirical Perspective* pp. 43–92. New York: Guildford Press.

Greer, C. (2004) Crime, media and community: Grief and virtual engagement in late modernity. In: J. Ferrell, K. Hayward, W. Morrison and M. Presdee (eds). *Cultural Criminology Unleashed.* London: Glasshouse Press, 97–108.

Gross, R. (2005) *Psychology: The Science of Mind and Behaviour.* London: Hodder and Arnold.

Gross, S.R., Jacoby, K., Matheson, D.J., Montgomery, N. and Patil, S. (2005) Exonerations in the United States 1989 through 2003. *The Journal of Criminal Law and Criminology,* 95, 523–60.

Gudjonsson, G.H. (2007) Investigative interviewing. In: T. Newburn, T. Williamson and A. Wright (eds) *Handbook of Criminal Investigation.* Cullompton: Willan, 466–92.

Gudjonsson, G.H. and Copson, G. (1997) The role of the expert in criminal investigation. In: J.L. Jackson and D. Bekerian (eds).

Offender Profiling: Theory, Research and Practice. Chichester: Wiley, 61–76.

Hafer, C.L. and Begue, L. (2005) Experimental research on just-world theory: Problems, developments, and future challenges. *Psychological Bulletin,* 131, 128–67.

Haney, C., Banks, W. C. and Zimbardo, P. G. (1973) *Study of Prisoners and Guards in a Simulated Prison* (Naval Research Reviews 9 (1–17)). Washington, DC: Office of Naval Research.

Harradine, S., Kodz, L., Lemetti, F. and Jones, B. (2004) *Defining and Measuring Anti-social Behaviour.* Home Office Practice and Development Report. London: Home Office.

Haste, H., Markoulis, D. and Helkama, K. (1998) Morality, wisdom and the life span. In: A. Demetriou, W. Doise and C. Van Lieshout (eds). *Life-span Developmental Psychology.* Chichester: Wiley.

Hastie, R. (1993) (ed) *Inside the Juror: The Psychology of Juror Decision Making.* Cambridge, MA: Cambridge University Press.

Hastie, R., Penrod, S.D. and Pennington, N. (1983) *Inside the Jury.* Cambridge: Harvard University Press.

Hatcher, R. and Hollin, C.R. (2005) The identification and management of anti-social and offending behaviour. In: J. Winstone and F. Pakes (Eds). *Community Justice: Issues for Probation and Criminal Justice.* Cullompton: Willan, 165-82.

Hayes, H. (2005) Assessing reoffending in restorative justice conferences. *Australian and New Zealand Journal of Criminology,* 38, 77–101.

Herrington, V. and Millie, A. (2006) Applying reassurance policing: Is it business as usual? *Policing and Society,* 16, 146–63.

HMP Wandsworth (2005) *HMP Wandsworth Prison Induction Manual.* London: HMP Wandsworth.

Hockley, W.E., Hemsworth, D.H. and Consoli, A. (1999) Shades of the mirror effect: recognition of faces with or without sunglasses. *Memory and Cognition,* 27, 128–38.

Hogarth, J. (1971) *Sentencing as a Human Process.* Toronto: University of Toronto Press.

Home Office (1998) *Speaking up for Justice.* London: Home Office.

Home Office (2003) *Together: Tackling Antisocial Behaviour: The One-day Count of Anti-social Behaviour.* London: Home Office.

Hood, R. (2002) *The Death Penalty: A Worldwide Perspective (3rd edition).* Oxford: Oxford University Press.

Huesmann, L.R. (1998) The role of social information processing and cognitive schemas in the acquisition and maintenance of habitual aggressive behaviour. In: R.G. Geen and E. Donnerstein (Eds). *Human Aggression: Theories, Research and Implications for Policy.* New York: Academic Press, 73–109.

Huesmann, L.R., Moise-Titus, J., Podolski, C.-L. and Eron, L.D. (2003) Longitudinal relations between children's exposure to TV violence and their aggressive and violent behaviour in young adulthood: 1977–1992. *Developmental Psychology,* 39, 201–221.

Huff, C.R., Rattner, A. and Sagarin, E. (1986) *Convicted but Innocent: Wrongful Conviction and Public Policy.* Thousand Oaks, California: Sage.

Human Rights Watch (2001) *Violence Against Women and "Honor" Crimes.* London: Human Rights Watch, April 6, 2001.

Ireland, J. (2004) Anger Management Therapy with young male offenders: An evaluation of treatment outcome. *Aggressive behaviour,* 30, 174–85.

Irving, B. (1980) *Police interrogation: A case study of current practice.* Research Study no. 2, Royal Commission on Criminal Procedure. London: HMSO.

It will take more than policing to curb gun crime (Leader). *The Observer,* 18 February 2007.

Iwasa, N. (1992) Postconventional reasoning and moral education in Japan. *Journal of Moral Education,* 21, 3–16.

Jackson, J.L. and Bekerian, D.A. (1997) (eds). Does offender profiling have a role to play? In: J.L. Jackson and D.A. Bekerian. *Offender Profiling: Theory, Research and Practice.* Chichester: Wiley, 1–8.

Jaffee, S.R., Caspi, A., Moffitt, T.E., Dodge, K.A., Rutter, M., Taylor, A. and Tully, L.A. (2005) Nature X nurture: genetic vulnerabilities interact with physical maltreatment to promote conduct problems. *Development and Psychopathology,* 17, 67–84.

Janis, I.L. (1972) *Victims of Groupthink.* Boston: Houghton Mifflin Company.

Johnston, D.K. (1988) Adolescents' solutions to dilemmas in fables: Two moral orientations – two problem-solving strategies. In C. Gilligan, J.V. Ward and J.M. Taylor (Eds). *Mapping the Moral Domain.* Cambridge, MA: Harvard University Press, 49–138.

Joy Tong, L.S. and Farrington, D.P. (2006) How effective is the 'Reasoning and rehabilitation programme in reducing reoffending? A meta-analysis of Evaluations in Four Countries. *Psychology, Crime and Law,* 12, 3–24.

Judicial and Court Statistics 2006 (2007) *Judicial and Court Statistics 2006.* London: HMSO, November 2007.

Kapardis, A. (1985) *Sentencing by English Magistrates as a Human Process.* Nicosia, Cyprus: Asselia Press.

Kapardis, A. (2003) *Psychology and Law: a Critical Introduction (2nd edition).* Cambridge: Cambridge University Press.

Kassin, S.M. and Wrightsman, L.S. (1985) Confession evidence. In: S.M. Kassin and L.S. Wrightsman (Eds.). *The Psychology of Evidence and Trial Procedure.* Beverly Hills, CA: Sage, 67–94.

Katz, A., Buchanan, A. and Bream, V. (2001) *Bullying in Britain: Testimonies from Teenagers.* London: Young Voice.

Katz, J. (1988) *The Seductions of Crime.* New York: Basic Books.

Kebbell, M.R. and Wagstaff, G.F. (1999) *Face value? Evaluating the Accuracy of Eyewitness Information.* Police Research Series Paper 102. London: Home Office.

Kelling, G.L., Pate, T., Dieckman, D. and Brown, C.E. (1974) *The Kansas City Preventive Patrol Experiment: A Summary Report*. Washington, DC: Police Foundation.

Kenrick, D.T. and MacFarlane, S.W. (1986) Ambient temperature and horn-honking: A field study of the heat/aggression relationship. *Environment and Behaviour*, 18, 179–91.

Kerstholt, J.H., Jansen, N.J.M., Van Amelsfoort, A.G. and Broeders, A.P.A. (2006) Earwitnesses: Effects of accent, retention and telephone. *Applied Cognitive Psychology*, 20, 187–97.

Kohlberg, L. (1984) *Essays on Moral Development: The Psychology of Moral Development, Vol. 2*. New York: Harper and Row.

Köhnken, G. (2004) Statement Validity Analysis and the 'detection of the truth'. In: P.A. Granhag and L.A. Strömwall (eds). *The Detection of Deception in Forensic Contexts*. Cambridge: Cambridge University Press, 41–63.

Lazer D. and Meyer, M. (2004) DNA and the Criminal Justice System: Consensus and Debate, in D. Lazer (ed) *DNA and the Criminal Justice System: The Technology of Justice*. Cambridge, MA: MIT Press, 357–90.

Le Bon, G. (1895) *The Crowd: A Study of the Popular Mind*. London: Transaction.

Lerner, M. J. (1980) *The Belief in a Just World: A Fundamental Delusion*. New York: Plenum Press.

Leyens, J.-P., Camino, L., Parke, R.D. and Berkowitz, L. (1975) Effects of movie violence on aggression in a field setting as a function of group dominance and cohesion. *Journal of Personality and Social Psychology*, 32, 346–60.

Loeber, R. and Farrington, D.P. (eds.) (2001) *Child Delinquents: Development, Intervention and Service Needs*. Thousand Oaks, CA: Sage.

Loftus, E.F. (1993) The reality of repressed memories. *American Psychologist*, 48, 518–37.

Loftus, E.F. and Ketcham, K. (1994) *The Myth of Repressed Memory: False Memories and Allegations of Sexual Abuse*. New York: St. Martin's Press.

Loftus, E.F. and Palmer, J.E. (1974) Reconstruction of automobile destruction: An example of the interaction between language and memory. *Journal of Verbal Learning and Verbal Behaviour*, 13, 585–9.

Loftus, E.F. and Pickrell, J.E. (1995) The formation of false memories. *Psychiatric Annals*, 25, 720–5.

Loftus, E.F., Loftus, G.R., and Messo, J. (1987) Some facts about 'weapon focus'. *Law and Human Behaviour*, 11, 55–62.

Lombroso, C. (1876) *L'Uomo delinquente*. Milan: Torin.

Lorenz, K. (1966) *On Aggression*. New York: Harcourt Brace.

Lösel, F. and Schmucker, M. (2005) The effectiveness of treatment for sexual offenders: A comprehensive meta-analysis. *Journal of Experimental Criminology*, 1, 117–46.

Lumet, S. (1957) *12 Angry Men*. Los Angeles: Orion Nova Productions.

Macfarlane, B.A. (1997) People who stalk people. *USB Law Review*, 31, 37–103.

MacLin, K.M. and Herrera, V. (2006) The criminal stereotype. *North American Journal of Psychology*, 8, 197–207.

Mandeville-Norden, R. and Beech, A. (2004) Community-based treatment of sex offenders. *Journal of Sexual Aggression*, 10, 193–214.

Marlatt, G.A. and Gordon, J.R. (eds.). (1985) *Relapse Prevention: Maintenance Strategies in the Treatment of Addictive Behaviours*. New York: Norton.

Marshall, T. (1999) *Restorative Justice: An Overview*. London: Home Office.

Marshall, W.L. (1989) Intimacy, loneliness and sexual offending. *Behavioural Research and Therapy*, 17, 491–503.

Mawby, R.I., Brunt, P. and Hambly, Z. (2000) Fear of crime among British holidaymakers. *British Journal of Criminology*, 40, 468–79.

McCabe, S. and Purves, R. (1974) *The Jury at Work*. Oxford: Blackwell.

McCrae, R. R. and Costa, P. T., Jr. (1999) A five-factor theory of personality. In: L.A. Pervin and O.P. John (Eds.) *Handbook of Personality: Theory and Research*. New York: Guildford, 139–53.

McCrae, R.R., Costa, P.T. Jr. and Ostendorf, F. (2000) Nature over nurture: Temperament, personality and lifespan development. *Journal of Personality and Social Psychology*, 78, 173–86.

McGuire, M. (2004) *Understanding Psychology and Crime*. Buckingham: Open University Press.

Mednick, S.A., Gabrielli, W.F. and Hutchings, B. (1984) Genetic influences in criminal convictions: Evidence from an adoption cohort. *Science*, 234, 891–4.

Meissner, C. and Brigham, J.C. (2001) Twenty years of investigating the own-race bias in memory for faces: A meta-analytic review. *Psychology, Public Policy and Law*, 7, 3–35.

Memon, A., Vrij, A. and Bull, R. (2003) *Psychology and Law: Truthfulness, Accuracy and Credibility (2nd edition)*. Chichester: Wiley.

Miers, D., Maguire, M., Goldie, S., Sharpe, K., Hale, C., Netten, A., Uglow, S., Doolin, K., Hallam, A., Enterkin, J. and Newburn, T. (2001) *An Exploratory Evaluation of Restorative Justice Schemes*. Home Office Crime Reduction Research Series Paper 9, London: Home Office.

Miller, J. D., and Lynam, D. R. (2001) Structural models of personality and their relation to. antisocial behavior: A meta-analysis. *Criminology*, 39, 765–98.

Miller, N.E. (1941) The Frustration-Aggression Hypothesis. *Psychological Review* 48, 337–42.

Milne, R. and Bull, R. (1999) *Investigative Interviewing: Psychology and Practice*. Chichester: Wiley.

Milne, R., Clare, I.C.H. and Bull, R (1999) Using the cognitive interview with adults with mild learning disabilities. *Psychology, Crime and Law*, 5, 81–99.

Ministry of Justice (2008) *Offenders on Community Sentences have Paid Back £33m in Unpaid Work this Year.* Ministry of Justice Press Release, 2 January 2008.

Mobius, M. and Rosenblat, T. (2006) Why beauty matters. *American Economic Review,* 96, 222–35.

Morris, J. (2006) *The National Reassurance Policing Programme: A ten site evaluation.* Home Office Findings, no. 273. London: Home Office.

Moscovici, S., Lage, E. and Naffrechoux, M. (1969) Influence of a consistent minority on the responses of a majority in a colour perception test. *Sociometry,* 32, 365–80.

Mowrer, O. H. (1947) On the dual nature of learning - a reinterpretation of "conditioning" and "problem solving". *Harvard Educational Review,* 17, 102–148.

Myhill, A. and Allen, J. (2002) *Rape and Sexual Assault on Women: The Extent and Nature of the Problem.* Home Office Research Study No. 237. London: Home Office.

Naeem, F., Bhatti, F., Pickering, R. and Kingdon, R. (2007) A controlled trial of the effectiveness of drug treatment & testing orders (DTTO) with standard care. *Journal of Substance Abuse,* 12, 253–65.

National Crime Faculty (1998) *A Practical Guide to Investigative Interviewing (2nd edition)* Bramshill: National Crime Faculty.

Newburn, T. (2007) *Criminology.* Cullompton: Willan.

Nicholas, S., Kershaw, C. and Walker, A. (2006) *Crime in England and Wales 2005/6.* Home Office: Research, Development and Statistics.

Nicholas, S., Povey, D., Walker, D. and Kershaw, C. (2005) *Crime in England and Wales 2004/5.* London: Home office. Available on: www.homeoffice.gov.uk/rds/pdfs05/hosb1105.pdf.

Ofcom (2006) *Communications Market Report 2005.* London: Ofcom.

Pakes, F. (2004) *Comparative Criminal Justice.* Cullompton: Willan.

Pakes, F. (2005) Under siege: The global faith of euthanasia and assisted suicide legislation. *European Journal of Crime, Criminal Law and Criminal Justice,* 13, 119–35.

Pakes, F. and Winstone, J. (2007) *Psychology and Crime: Understanding and Tackling Offender Behaviour.* Cullompton: Willan.

Palmer, E. (2003) *Offending Behaviour: Moral Reasoning, Criminal Conduct and the Rehabilitation of Offenders.* Cullompton: Willan.

Palmer, E. (2005) The relationship between moral reasoning and aggression, and the implications for practice. *Psychology, Crime and Law,* 11, 353–61.

Palmer, E. and Hollin, C. (1998) A comparison of patterns of moral development in young offenders and non-offenders. *Legal and Criminological Psychology,* 3, 225–35.

Palmer, E. and Hollin, C. (2000) The interrelations of sociomoral reasoning, perceptions of own parenting and attribution of intent with self-reported delinquency. *Legal and Criminological Psychology,* 5, 201–218.

Parliamentary Office of Science and Technology (2006) *The National DNA Database. POST Postnote 258.* London: POST.

Pavlov, I. (1927) *Conditioned Reflexes.* Oxford: Oxford University Press.

Pennington, N. and Hastie, R. (1992) Explaining the evidence: tests of the story model for juror decision making, *Journal of Personality and Social Psychology,* 62, 189–206.

Pennington, N. and Hastie, R. (1993) The story model for juror decision making. In: R. Hastie (Ed.). *Inside the Juror: The Psychology of Juror Decision Making.* Cambridge, MA: Cambridge University Press, 192–221.

Philippon, A., Cherryman, J., Bull, R. and Vrij, A. (2007) Earwitness identification performance: The effect of language, target, deliberate strategies and indirect measures. *Applied Cognitive Psychology,* 21, 539–50.

Plomin, R. and Asbury, K. (2005) Nature *and* nurture: Genetic and environmental influences on behavior. *Annals of the American Academy of Political and Social Science,* 600, 86–94.

Postmes, T. and Spears, R. (1998) Deindividuation and antinormative behaviour: A meta-analysis. *Psychological Bulletin,* 123, 238–59.

Powell, C.L. and Bamber, D. (2007) Drug treatment in the criminal justice system: Lessons learnt from offenders on DTTOs. *Drugs: Eduction, Prevention and Policy,* 14, 333–45.

Pratt, T.C., Cullen, F.T., Blevins, K.R., Daigle, L. and Unnever, J.D. (2002) The relationship of attention deficit Hyperactivity Disorder to crime and delinquency: a meta-analysis. *International Journal of Police Science and Management,* 4, 344–60.

Prentky, R. A., Lee, A. F. S., Knight, R. A. and Cerce, D. (1997) Recidivism rates among child molesters and rapists: A methodological analysis. *Law and Human Behavior,* 21, 635–59.

R. v Turnbull and others (1977) QB 224; (1976) 3 AVE R 549 at 549–550.

Raine, A., Buchsbaum, M. and LaCasse, L. (1997) Brain abnormalities in murderers indicated by positron emission tomography. *Biological Psychiatry,* 42, 495–508.

Ressler, R. K., Burgess, A. W. and Douglas, J. E. (1988) *Sexual Homicide: Patterns and Motives.* Lexington, MA: Lexington.

Ressler, R.K. and Shachtman, T. (1992) *Whoever Fights Monsters.* London: Simon and Schuster.

Robinson, D. and Porporino, F.J. (2001) Programming in cognitive skills: The reasoning and rehabilitation programme. In: C.R. Hollin (Ed.) *Handbook of Offender Assessment and Treatment.* Chichester: Wiley, 179–93.

Ross, D.F., Hopkins, S., Hanson, E., Lindsay, R., Eslinger, T. and Hazen, K. (1994) The impact of protective shields and videotape testimony on conviction rates in trials of child sexual abuse. *Law and Human Behavior,* 18, 553–66.

Ross, R.R., Fabiano, E.A. and Ewles, C.D. (1988) Reasoning and rehabilitation. *International Journal of Offender Therapy and Comparative Criminology,* 32, 29–35.

Russell, S. (1997) Castration of repeat sexual offenders: An international comparative analysis. *Houston Journal of International Law*, 19, 425–59.

Salisbury, H. and Upson, A. (2004) *Ethnicity, Victimisation and Worry about Crime: Findings from the 2001/02 and 2002/03 British Crime Surveys*. London: Home Office.

Savage, S.P. and Milne, B. (2007) Miscarriages of justice. In: T. Newburn, T. Williamson and A. Wright (Eds.) *Handbook of Criminal Investigation*. Cullompton: Willan, 610–627.

Schank, R.C. and Abelson, R.P. (1977) *Scripts, Plans, Goals and Understanding*. Hillsdale, NJ, US: Lawrence Erlbaum.

Scott, H. (2003) Stranger danger: Explaining women's fear of crime. *Western Criminology Review*, 4, 203-214.

Sentencing Statistics 2006 (2007) *Sentencing Statistics 2006*. Ministry of Justice: London: Home Office/Ministry of Justice.

Shapland, J., Atkinson, A., Atkinson, H., Chapman, B., Colledge, E., Dignan, J., Howes, M., Johnstone, J., Robinson, G. and Sorsby, A. (2006) *Restorative Justice in Practice: Findings from the Second Phase of the Evaluation of Three Schemes*. Home Office RDS Findings 274. London: Home Office.

Sheridan, L. and Davies, G.M. (2001) Stalking: The elusive crime. *Legal and Criminological Psychology*, 6, 133–47.

Sigall, H. and Ostrove, N. (1975) Beautiful but dangerous: Effects of offender attractiveness and nature of crime on juridic judgement. *Journal of Personality and Social Psychology*, 31, 410–14.

Singleton, N., Meltzer, H. and Gatward, R. (1998) *Psychiatric Morbidity among Prisoners in England and Wales*. London: Office for National Statistics.

Skinner, B.F. (1938) *The Behaviour of Organisms*. New York: Appleton.

Social Exclusion Unit (2002) *Reducing Reoffending by Ex-offenders*. London: Social Exclusion Unit.

Sommers, S.R. (2006) On racial diversity and group decision making: Identifying multiple effects of racial composition on jury deliberations. *Journal of Personality and Social Psychology*, 2006, 90, 597–612.

Stanko, E.A. (1992) The case of fearful women: gender, personal safety and fear of crime. *Women and Criminal Justice*, 4, 117–35.

Steblay, N.M. (1997) Social influence in eyewitness recall: A meta-analytic review of lineup instruction effects. *Law and Human Behaviour*, 21, 283—98.

Steblay, N.M., Dysart, J., Fulero, S. and Lindsay, R.C.L. (2001) Eyewitness accuracy rates in sequential and simultaneous lineup presentations: a meta-analytic comparison. *Law and Human Behaviour*, 25, 459–74.

Stephen Lawrence Inquiry (1999) *Report of an inquiry by Sir William Macpherson of Cluny*. London: HMSO, Cm 4262-I.

Stewart, J.E. (1980) Defendants' attractiveness as a factor in the outcome of criminal trials: An observational study. *Journal of Applied Social Psychology*, 10, 348–61.

Sykes, G. and Matza, D. (1957) Techniques of neutralization: A theory of delinquency. *American Sociological Review*, 22, 664–70.

Tajfel, H., Billig, M.G. and Bundy, R.P. (1971) Social categorisation and intergroup behaviour. *European Journal of Social Psychology*, 1, 149–78.

Thorndike, E. L. (1920) A constant error on psychological rating. *Journal of Applied Psychology*, 4, 25–29.

Tjaden, P. and Thoennes, N. (1998) *Stalking In America: Findings From The National Violence Against Women Survey* Washington, D.C: U.S. Department of Justice, National Institute of Justice.

Townley, L. and Ede, R. (2004) *Forensic Practice in Criminal Cases.* London: The Law Society.

Turvey, B. (2002) *Criminal Profiling: An Introduction to Behavioural Evidence Analysis (2nd edition).* San Diego: Academic Press.

United Nations (2004) *Working towards the elimination of crimes against women committed in the name of honour:* Report of the Secretary-General. Available on line: http://www.unhchr.ch/huridocda/huridoca.nsf/AllSymbols/985168F508EE799FC1256C52002AE5A9/%24File/N0246790.pdf.

Vrij, A. (2000) *Detecting Lies and Deceit: The Psychology of Lying and its Implications for Professional Practice.* Chichester: Wiley.

Vrij, A. (2005) Criteria-Based Content Analysis: A qualitative review of the first 37 studies. *Psychology, Public Policy and the Law*, 11, 3–41.

Vrij, A. and Granhag, P-A. (2005) Detection deception. In: N. Brewer and K.D. Williams (Eds) *Psychology and Law: An Empirical Perspective.* New York: Guildford Press, 43–92.

Wagenaar, W.A. and Van der Schrier, J. (1994) *Face Recognition as a Function of Distance and Illumination: A Practical Test of Use in the Courtroom.* Paper presented at the fourth European Conference of Law and Psychology, Barcelona, Spain, April 1994.

Walby, S. and Allen, J. (2004) *Domestic Violence, Sexual Assault and Stalking: Findings from the British Crime Survey.* London: Home Office Research, Development and Statistics Directorate.

Wall, D.S. (2007) *Cybercrime: The Transformation of Crime in the Information Age.* Cambridge: Polity Press.

Walker, A. Kershaw, C. and Nicholas, S. (2006) *Crime in England and Wales 2005/06.* London: Home Office. Available online: http://www.homeoffice.gov.uk/rds/pdfs06/hosb1206.pdf.

Welchman, L. and Hossain, S. (2006) Introduction: Honour, Rights and Wrongs. In: L. Welchman, L. and S. Hossain (Eds.) *Honour: Crimes, Paradigms and Violence Against Women.* London: Zed books, 1–21.

Wells, G.L. (1978) Applied eyewitness testimony research: system variables and estimator variables. *Journal of Personality and Social Psychology*, 36, 1546–57.

Wells, G.L. (1984) The psychology of lineup identifications. *Journal of Applied Social Psychology*, 14, 89–103.

Wells, G.L. and Olson, E. A. (2003) Eyewitness testimony. *Annual Review of Psychology*, 54, 277–95.

West, D. and D. Farrington. (1973) *Who Becomes Delinquent?* London: Heinemann.

Whitehead, C.M.E., Stockdale, J.E. and Razzu, G. (2003) *The Economic and Social Costs of Anti-social Behaviour: A Review*. London: London School of Economics.

Whittington, R. and Wykes, T. (1994) Aversive stimulation by staff and violence by psychiatric patients. *British Journal of Clinical Psychology*, 35, 11–20.

Wilczynski, F.P. and Morris, A. (1993) Parents who kill their children. *Criminal Law Review*, 31–6.

Williams, R. and Johnson, P. (2005) Inclusiveness, effectiveness and intrusiveness: Issues in the developing uses of DNA profiling in support of criminal investigations. *Journal of Law and Medical Ethics*, 33, 545–558.

Wilson, D., Sharp, C. and Patterson, A. (2006) *Young People and Crime: Findings from the 2005 Offending, Crime and Justice Survey*. London: Home Office. Available on line: http://www.homeoffice.gov.uk/rds/pdfs06/hosb1706.pdf.

Womack, S. (2007) *TV toddlers 'become aggressive'*. Daily Telegraph, 8 May 2007.

Wright, D.B., Ost, J. and French, C.C. (2006) Recovered and false memories. *The Psychologist*, 19, 352–5.

Young, J. (1988) Risk of crime and fear of crime: A realist critique of survey-based assumptions. In: M. Maguire and J. Pointing (eds.) *Victims of crime: A new deal*. Milton Keynes: Open University Press, 164–76.

Young, J. (2004) Voodoo criminology and the numbers game. In: J. Ferrell, K. Hayward, W. Morrison and M. Presdee (Eds). *Cultural Criminology Unleashed*. London: Glasshouse Press, 14–27.

Zillman, D., Hoyt, J. L. and Day, K. D. (1974) Strength and duration of the effect of aggressive, violent and erotic communications on subsequent aggressive behaviors. *Communication Research*, 1, 286–306.

Zillman, D., Katcher, A.J. and Milavsky, B. (1972) Excitation transfer from physical exercise to subsequent aggressive behavior. *Journal of Experimental Social Psychology*, 8, 247–59.

Zimbardo, P. (1969) The human choice: Individuation, reason and order vs. deindividuation, impulse and chaos. In. W.J. Arnold and D. Levine (Eds). *Nebraska Symposium on Motivation*. Lincoln: University of Nebraska Press, 237–307.

Zimbardo, P.G. (1973) On the ethics of intervention in human psychological research with special reference to the 'Stanford Prison Experiment'. *Cognition*, 2, 243–255.

Index